Rediscovery & Restoration

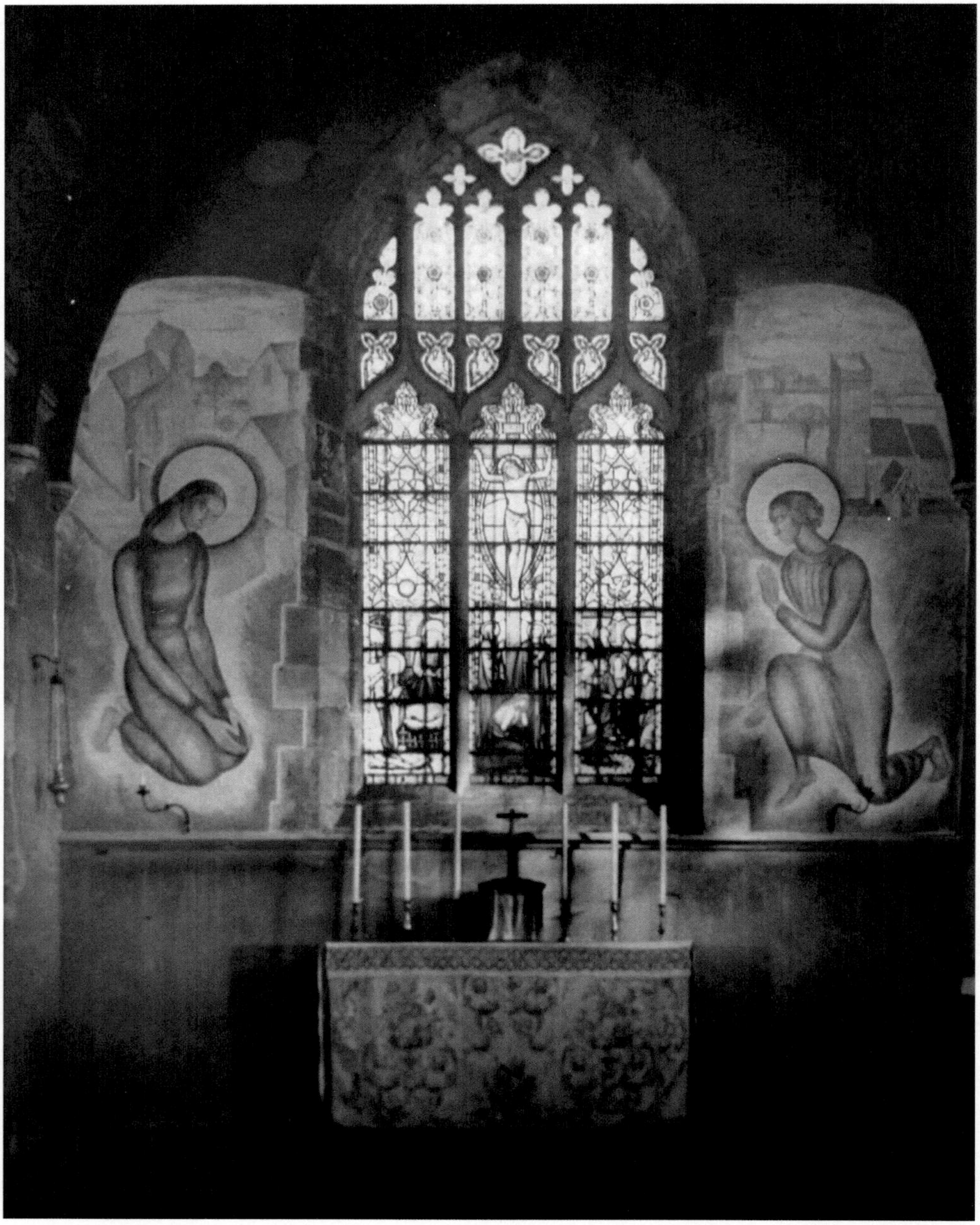

St. Martin's Church 'Annunciation' mural at completion, November 1946 – from original photograph by Ronald Hunt A.R.P. Studio Vaughan Leicester

REDISCOVERY & RESTORATION

Murals by Evelyn Gibbs at St Martin's Church, Bilborough

Pauline Lucas

Shoestring Press

Printed by imprintdigital
Upton Pyne, Exeter
www.imprintdigital.net

Typeset by narrator
www.narrator.me.uk
info@narrator.me.uk
033 022 300 39

Published by Shoestring Press
19 Devonshire Avenue, Beeston, Nottingham, NG9 1BS
(0115) 925 1827
www.shoestringpress.co.uk

Cover image: Interior of St. Martin's with Joy and Saskia Huning

First published 2015

ISBN 978-1-910323-24-3

ACKNOWLEDGMENTS

The purpose of this book is to report the momentous rediscovery, conservation and restoration of the mural of the 'Annunciation' in a small medieval church on the outskirts of Nottingham and to relate this mural by Evelyn Gibbs to the rest of her artistic career. Because the mural is in two sections separated by the imposing East Window of the church, I use 'murals' and the terms 'Wall Decorations' and 'Wall Paintings' in this account.

This book follows on from my earlier research into the career of Evelyn Gibbs which resulted in the publication of *Evelyn Gibbs, Artist and Traveller*. I am indebted to the late Sir Hugh Willatt, the artist's husband, for his invaluable help in providing access to crucial documentary material, notebooks, photographs and catalogues.

Many people have been involved in organising, funding, re-building and restoring the church and its murals. Hilary Wheat, Churchwarden, led the entire project, keenly supported by the Rev. Amanda Cartwright, gaining funding from several church trusts and in particular from the Heritage Lottery Fund. Architect Bruce Bradley and construction teams were responsible for considerable capital work on the fabric of the church before the sensitive conservation and recovery of the paintings could be started by Tobit Curteis Associates and Huning Decorations. For this achievement the restoration has been given the 2015 John Betjeman Award by the Society for the Preservation of Ancient Buildings (SPAB).

My thanks go to Narrator for expert work in typesetting and designing. For encouraging me to write about the history and background to the mural by Evelyn Gibbs I wish to thank my publisher.

The reproductions of paintings, drawings and prints are from the Estate of Evelyn Gibbs, private collections and by permission of the Imperial War Museum, Nottingham City Museums & Galleries and Bradford Art Galleries & Museums.

Photographs of the restoration and the murals themselves have been taken by members of the project team, by Hilary Wheat and Tobit Curteis to all of whom I offer my warm thanks.

For Amanda, Sam, and Macayla

CONTENTS

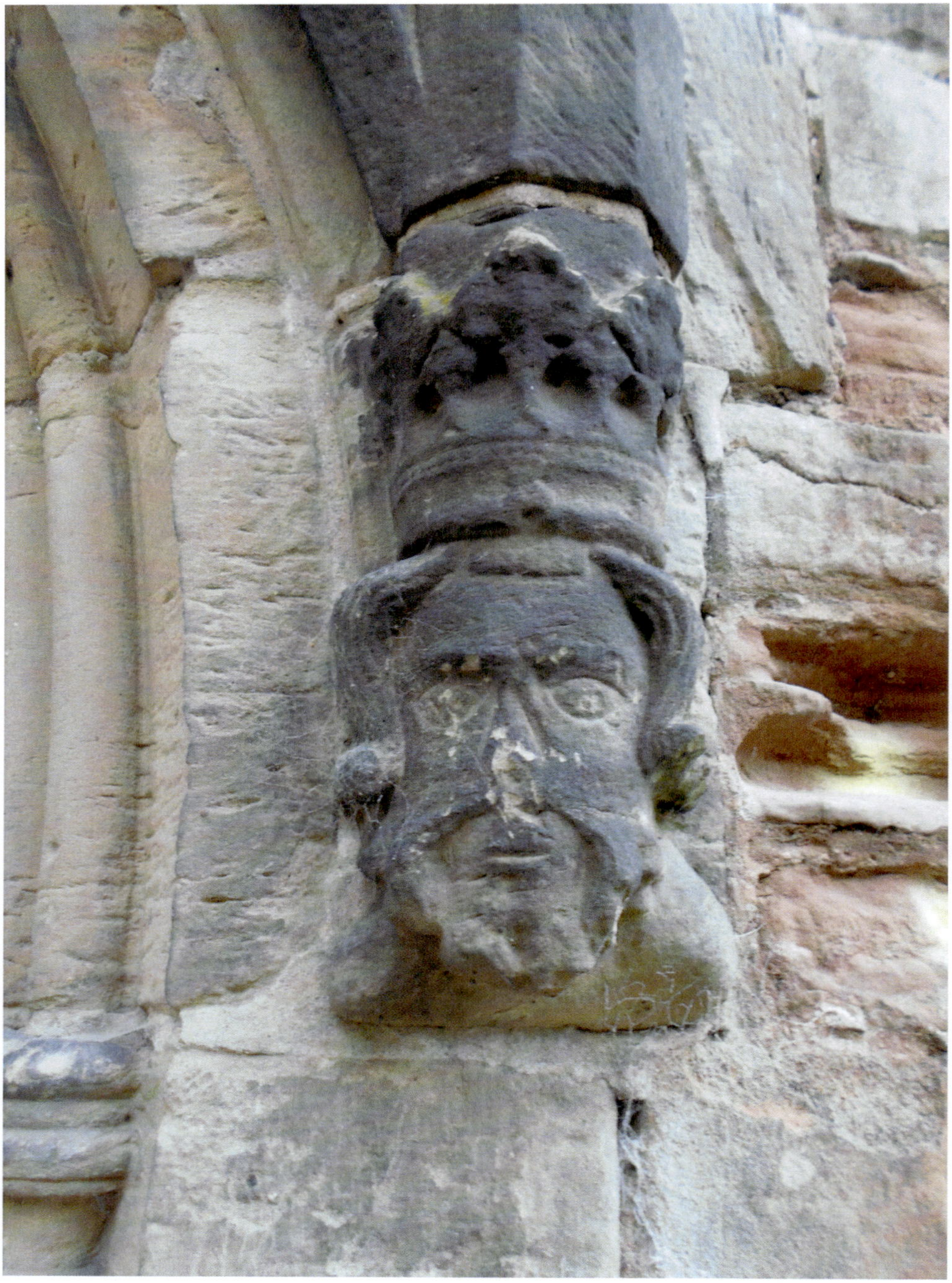

St. Martin's church porch, carved head of Edward III

I INTRODUCTION

The church of St. Martin of Tours, dating from the middle years of the 14th century, stands on a knoll at the heart of the former village of Bilborough, some four miles from the centre of Nottingham. Like most villages in the area it comprised a medieval church, a farm, a few houses, some cottages and a nearby mansion, Broxtowe Hall, with its sizeable estate. But with the development of coal-mining, quarrying and other industries in the 18th and 19th centuries around these Nottinghamshire villages, Bilborough in particular began to lose its separate identity and in the 20th century, after two world wars, large housing estates had spread to encroach on the former farmland and, in so doing, hide the older central parts of its village. A busy main road now by-passes the lane leading to St. Martin's church and its surrounding buildings. Motorists and bus-passengers speeding on their daily journeys could have no idea of the historic gem to be found down that lane.

This is how Nikolaus Pevsner (Nottinghamshire, The Buildings of England, 2nd edition) describes the church. "Essentially a late C14 church (see the windows in nave and chancel, and also the handsome s porch with a crocketed ogee niche (over the entrance) restored in 1887-9 by J.E. Newbury. W tower a later medieval replacement of one of the same date....Church extended in 1972." All true as far as it goes though nothing is explained about the 1972 extension.

Pevsner's account of the church leaves much to add. There had been many restorations to the fabric of the church over the centuries, including considerable work in the 19th century on at least two occasions, in 1833 and in a major way in 1887-9, when, under J.E.Newbury, repairs to the roof of the chancel included the addition of a finely carved barrel vault ceiling, decorated with bosses of floral design. It remained an attractive though modest example of medieval and 19th century building skills, with an East Window built in the perpendicular style, whose 19th century glass is believed to have come from All Saints Church, Strelley. The fine porch has carved heads of King Edward III and his Queen, Philippa of Hernault, on either side of the arched south entrance. By the 20th century the walls were bare, any earlier wall paintings having been defaced or removed during the Reformation and eventually replaced by tidier Victorian commemorative plaques and by the impressive late 16th century alabaster memorial to Sir Edmund Helwys of Broxtowe Hall.

II THE TWENTIETH CENTURY

However one remarkable addition was made in the mid twentieth century, when wall paintings were commissioned by the current rector, Father Marshall. The artist chosen to make them was the highly accomplished War Artist, Evelyn Gibbs. It was no doubt in a spirit of determined optimism after the difficulties and hardship of the war years, that Father Marshall made this inspired decision at a time of continued austerity. It must have entranced his congregation to witness vivid new works of art in their old church.

But time passed, and by the 1970s an expanding congregation from the nearby housing estates suggested the need for a larger church with community facilities. In 1972 the new rector Father Derek Shewring, decided on a plan to build an extension on the north side of the church by demolishing one wall of the chancel in order to create a modern open area for seating and a central position for the altar. This meant that the functional part of the church was now at right angles to the old church nave and separated from it by a thick curtain providing a thermal buffer between old and new. A pine ceiling was installed, extending across the chancel and over the newly created seating area, completely hiding the upper two thirds of the paintings and the former east window. To complete the alterations, the east window glass was smashed and the whole window bricked in. Then, since the altar had been removed from below, it was decided to paint out the rest of the mural with several coats of emulsion paint. The result of this highly unusual and destructive modernisation was the effective disappearance of a medieval church, with no glimpse or indication that anything of importance lay above the new ceiling. Now the church had an exceptionally stark entrance on its north side. Two large metal doors, industrial in appearance, set in an expanse of pale brickwork, provided the entrance to a foyer and the community rooms with a door leading to the new worship space beyond, whilst the traditional porch on the south of the church was unused and neglected.

Understandably, by the early 21st century the congregation had become well used to its warm church and its adaptability for all sorts of functions while the older members had all but forgotten the previous interior with its striking mural and cold drafts. However there was mounting concern about the dilapidation of the historic nave and tower. Churchwardens and architects voiced their anxieties. The tower was in desperate need of repairs but it was to be electricians working high above the pine ceiling in the chancel who noticed the upper parts of the painting of the 'Annunciation' and photographed them for the current churchwarden, setting off a whole chain of events which culminated in their restoration, together with the entire historic church in late 2014.

III MURALS/WALL PAINTINGS

How was it that these murals* came to be painted in 1946? The answer lies in the presence of a dedicated group of artists, who offered their skills to the public, and to their founder, Evelyn Gibbs, art education lecturer, painter and printmaker, who had been evacuated to Nottingham with her Goldsmiths' College students at the outbreak of war. Evelyn Gibbs was in mid-career with impressive training years behind her. Born in Liverpool in 1905, she won scholarships, first from Liverpool's City School of Art to London's Royal College of Art, to study etching and engraving, and then with the prestigious Prix de Rome, she was enabled to spend two years at the British School at Rome, mingling with other artists, classicists and archaeologists, studying, travelling and developing her art.

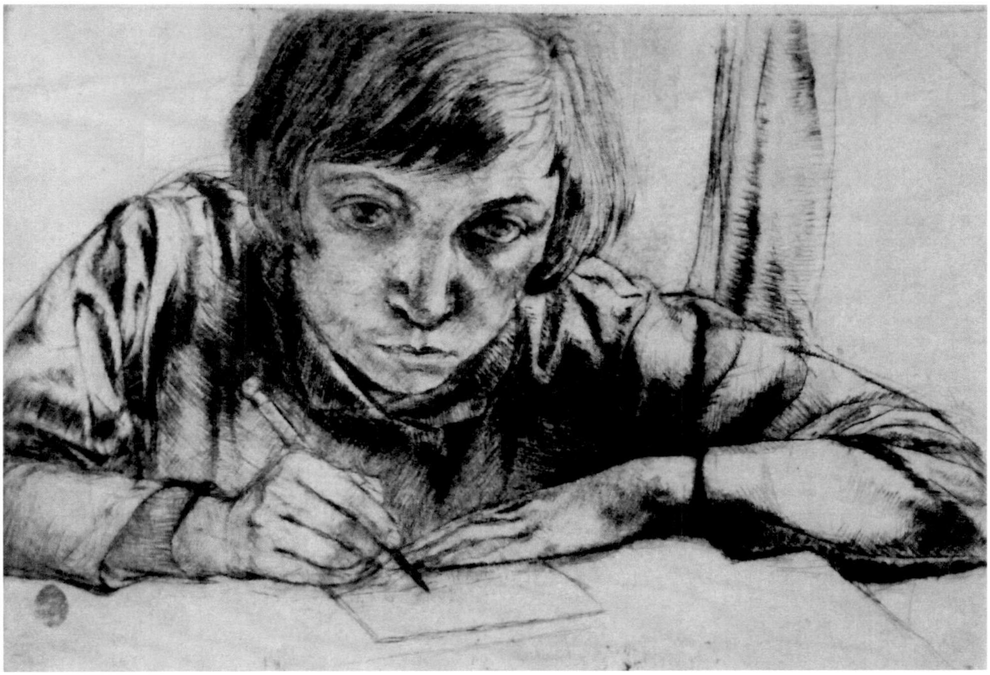

'Self Portrait' drypoint 1927

During the 1930s there were several exhibitions of her print works and paintings in London galleries, but to earn her living she became an art teacher whose remarkable methods and enthusiasm resulted in invitations to contribute to art teaching journals. Her book, *'The Teaching of Art in Schools, an Illustrated Description of Children's Imaginative Painting & its Effect on Craft'* published in 1934 by Williams & Norgate Ltd. became an admired and widely used manual for teachers, warmly praised for its stimulating and

* In fact the 'Annunciation' is one mural design but two separate paintings on either side of a window. The terms wall painting and wall decoration are equally valid.

practical qualities. (It was reprinted several times and a new edition came out in 1957.) By the time she arrived in Nottingham Gibbs was a respected authority in the field of Child Art and the teaching of the subject. She was appointed as a lecturer to teach students at Goldsmiths' College as a result of her expertise.

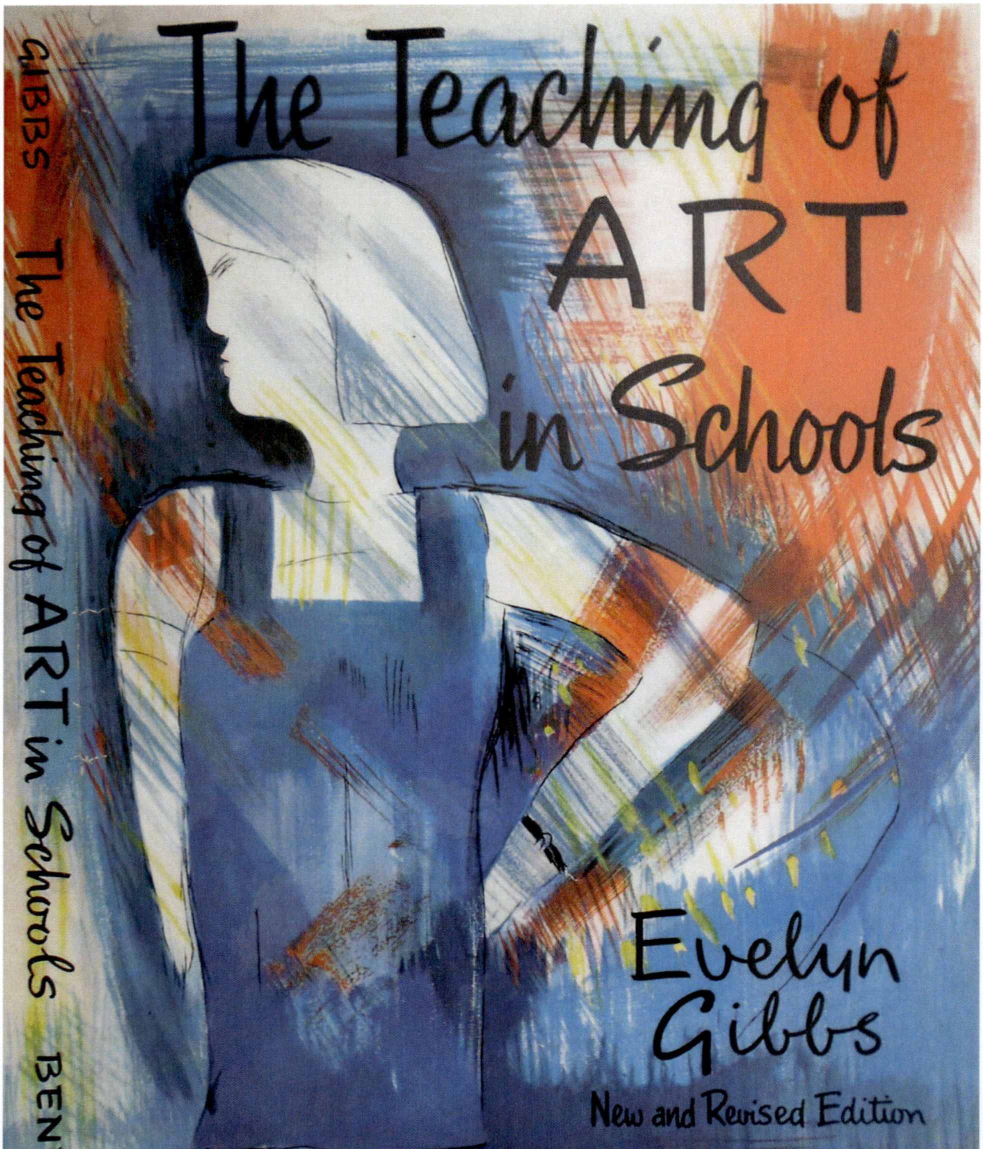

'The Teaching of Art in Schools', 1957 edition

IV WAR

In late August 1939, Evelyn Gibbs and her artist friend Elisabeth Vellacott had made a hasty retreat from France after a sketching holiday. Impending war meant evacuations from London of school children, their schools and most educational institutions. All kinds of people were similarly removed from their familiar surroundings and friends and directed to remote parts of the country to protect them from the expected enemy bombing. Gibbs and her colleagues at Goldsmiths' College were to be sent, for their own safety, to Nottingham, where the University College, as it was then, had allocated Hugh Stewart Hall, on the campus, for their use as teaching and living space until other billets could be found. As the newcomers settled into their unfamiliar surroundings other links and friendships were formed. Goldsmiths' College lecturers in Drama, Art and Music met their counterparts in the city, particularly in the theatre, where the arts came together. In addition to evacuees from London there were refugees from Spain and middle Europe, often distinguished artists and musicians fleeing from Fascism. The Cooperative Arts Theatre and the WEA, Workers' Education Authority, brought many of these talents together.

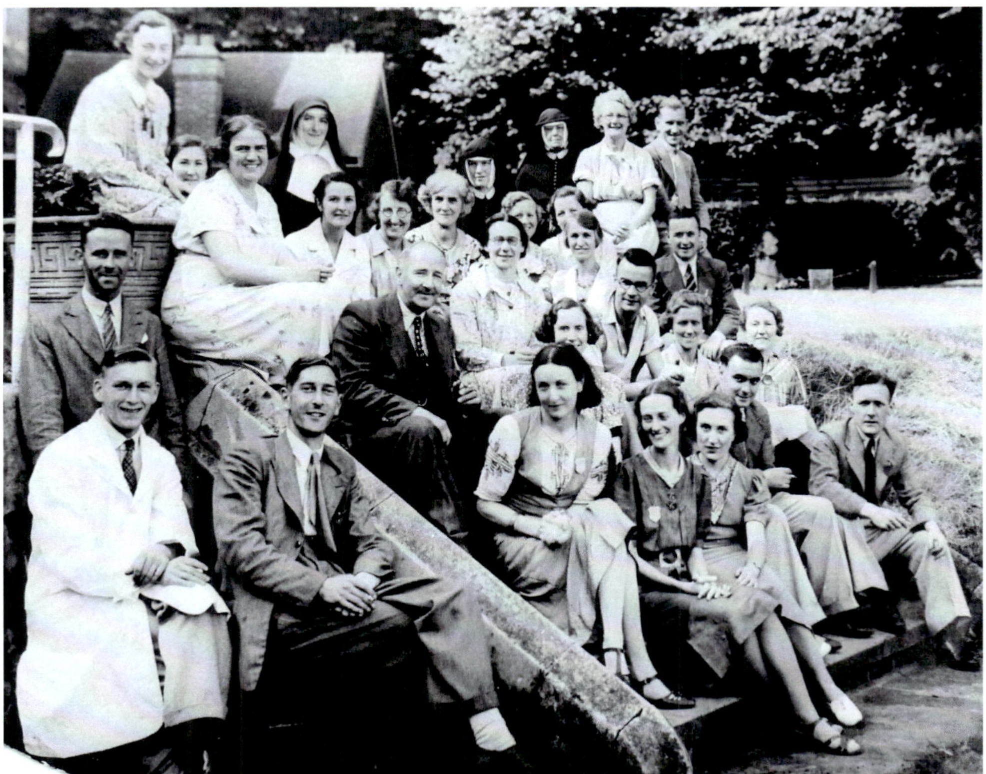

Goldsmiths' College teaching staff – Gibbs third from left, at centre, seated on steps – date and place unknown

Once established in Nottingham Evelyn Gibbs began to take on many important and demanding roles in addition to her teaching. The 'War Effort' was much in evidence in the city: local factories were taken over for munitions work; the Castle Museum, having been requisitioned by the military, was closed for the duration of the war. Gibbs herself was commissioned by the War Artists' Advisory Committee (via the Government Ministry of Information) to make drawings of women lab technicians in a Blood Transfusion Unit and also of women working on munitions at the Raleigh bicycle factory, now referred to as the 'Gun Factory.' For this she had been given an official permit to enter the factory as, under war-time restrictions, outsiders were prohibited. In 1943, she was further commissioned to make a painting of a W.V.S. 'swop shop' in Leicester, where mothers brought and exchanged children's clothing under the supervision of volunteering WVS ladies. The resulting painting titled 'The WVS Clothing Exchange' can be seen at the Imperial War Museum, in London, together with her other war drawings. *The Leicester Evening Mail* newspaper ran an article and photographed the scene

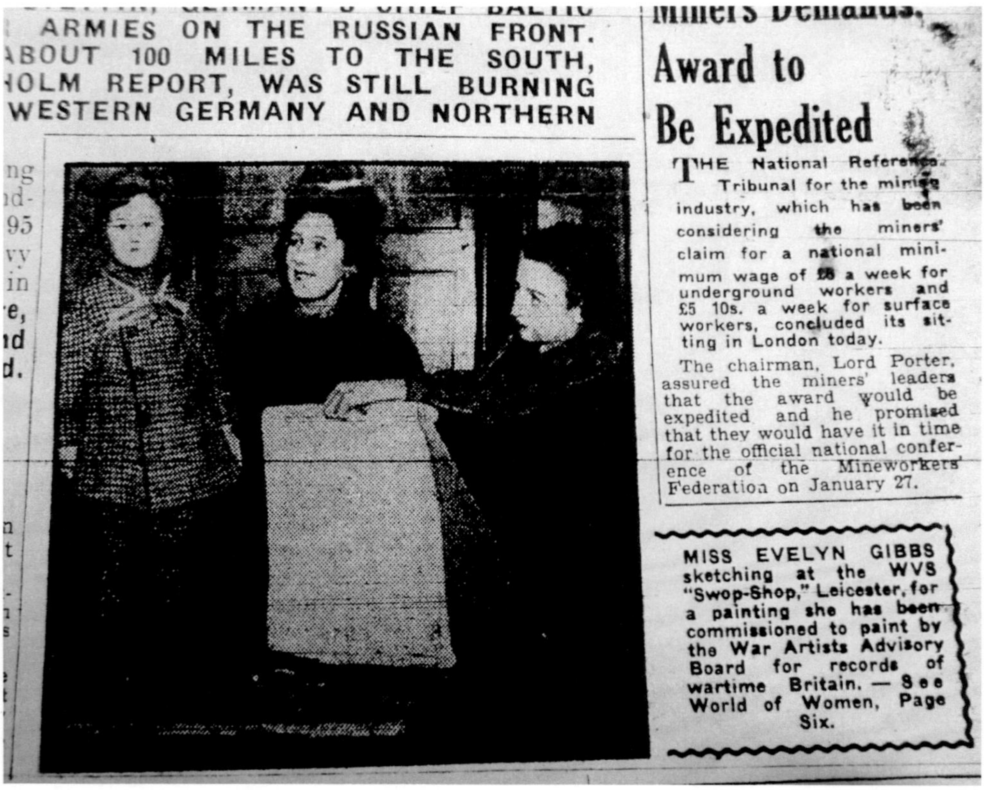

ARMIES ON THE RUSSIAN FRONT. ABOUT 100 MILES TO THE SOUTH, HOLM REPORT, WAS STILL BURNING WESTERN GERMANY AND NORTHERN

Award to Be Expedited

THE National Reference Tribunal for the mining industry, which has been considering the miners' claim for a national minimum wage of £6 a week for underground workers and £5 10s. a week for surface workers, concluded its sitting in London today.

The chairman, Lord Porter, assured the miners' leaders that the award would be expedited and he promised that they would have it in time for the official national conference of the Mineworkers' Federation on January 27.

MISS EVELYN GIBBS sketching at the WVS "Swop-Shop," Leicester, for a painting she has been commissioned to paint by the War Artists Advisory Board for records of wartime Britain. — See World of Women, Page Six.

Evelyn Gibbs drawing at WVS centre, Leicester Evening Mail

as Evelyn Gibbs made sketches on a huge pad surrounded by mothers and children. Several drawings of individual children and mothers were afterwards combined in a harmonious composition painted in muted greenish-blues, ochres and magentas, where

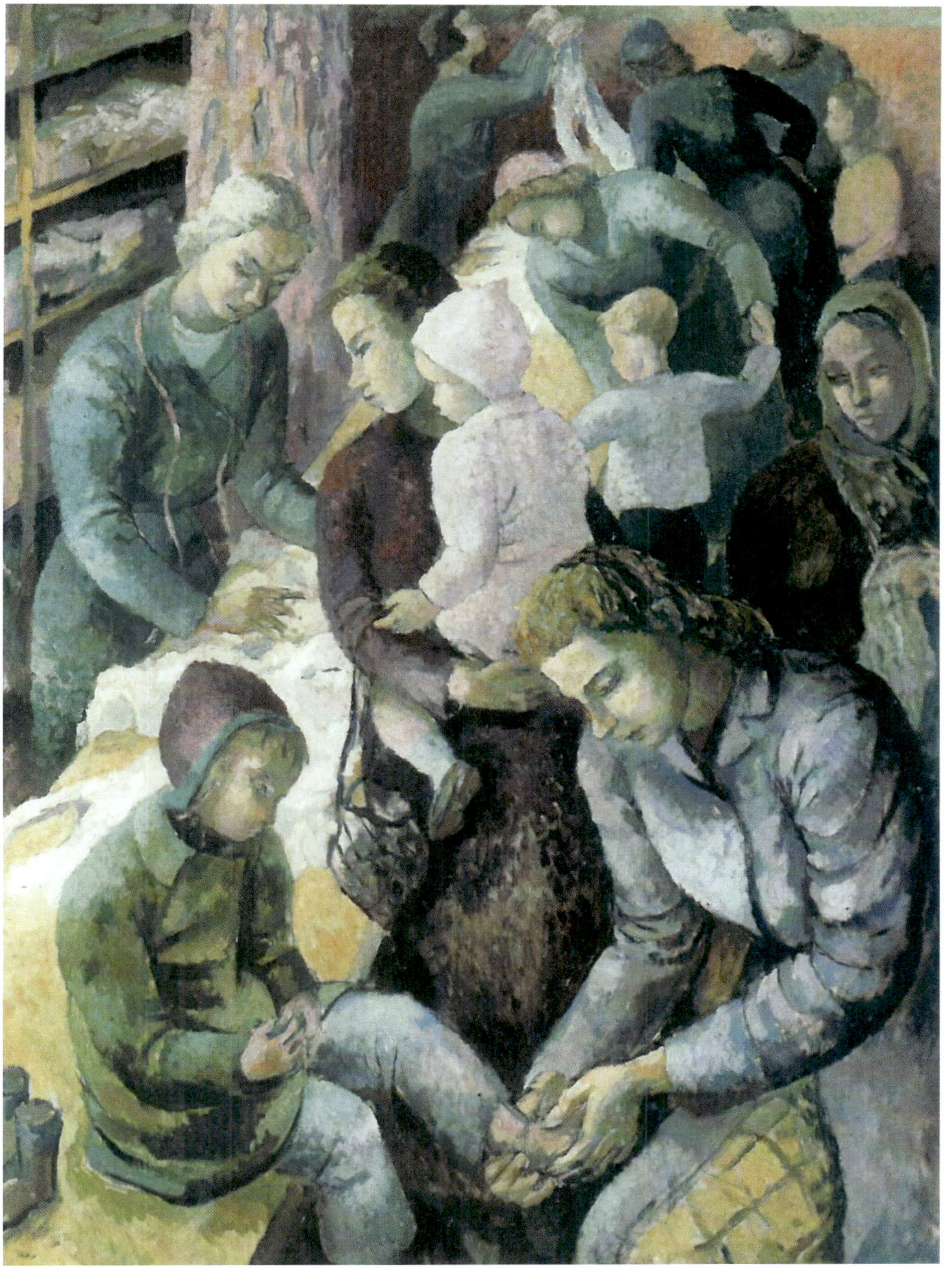

'WVS Clothing Exchange', oils on canvas, 1943, © Imperial War Museum (IWM) London

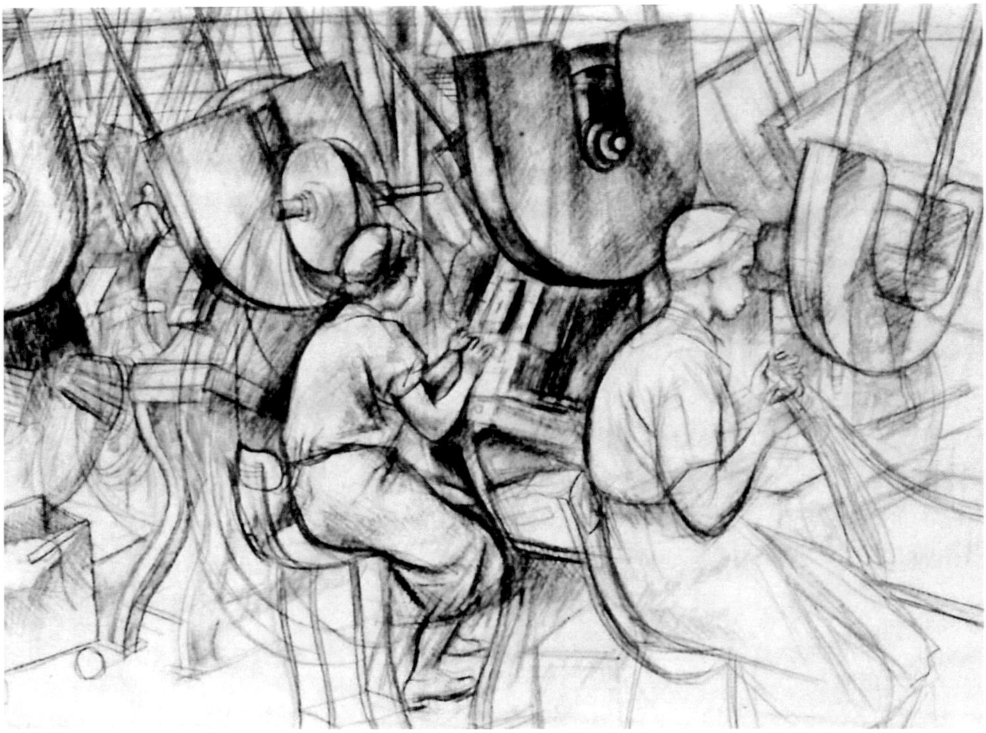

'Women at Work (munitions) Raleigh Works Nottingham', charcoal, ink and conté, 1943, Bradford Art Galleries and Museums

the rhythmical flow of movements of figures creates a scene of contented activity.

Many of the foremost British artists were similarly engaged in commissions to draw or paint aspects of wartime, though women artists were allocated only scenes of women's work, voluntary or paid. Another more famous Nottingham artist, Dame Laura Knight, received a number of commissions, among the best known of which is the painting 'Ruby Loftus Screwing a Breech-ring,' 1943, also in the collection of the I.W.M. In 1946, at the time when Gibbs was at work on the St. Martin's murals, Laura Knight was commissioned to paint a most remarkable record of the Nuremberg Trials of Nazi war criminals, then taking place in Germany, the only instance when a woman had been given such a role. Actually there were many women war artists whose work is still little known despite the high quality of their work. These include three prolific and successful artists, Evelyn Dunbar, Mary Adshead and Olga Lehmann, all three muralists. At least twelve women artists received commissions and many more, whether acknowledged or not made artwork during the war. Olga Lehmann's murals were painted in underground storage tunnels near Bath, inaccessible to most. Inevitably male war artists are much better known and celebrated. Most people will have heard of Paul Nash, Stanley Spencer and Eric Ravilious, all well represented in our National collections.

V THE MIDLAND REGIONAL DESIGNERS' GROUP

In early 1943, in the midst of all this activity, Evelyn Gibbs took it on herself to organise an artists' group based in Nottingham, with a committee headed by the already famous Laura Knight as President and including, as patrons, important local figures: Vivian de Sola Pinto, H. Wortley and William Davies, Professors at Nottingham; the Principals of Leicester, Loughborough and Mansfield Colleges of Art and Trevor Thomas, Director of Leicester Art Gallery. At first named the Nottingham Regional Designers' Group, it was soon renamed the Midland Regional Designers' Group, to include artists from Leicester, Loughborough, Mansfield and Derby. (As the Midland Group, it was to flourish for many years, running ever larger galleries, until its closure in 1987.)

After an inaugural exhibition in the summer of 1943, *Art for All,* they advertised their work through a leaflet offering *'Travelling Exhibitions and Wall Decorations for Factories, Canteens, Halls and Rest Centres'*, to enliven the drab war-time scene for local people and the servicemen and women training in the area, and also to provide socially useful occupation for artists. In so doing they were following a scheme promoted by the A.I.A. (the Artists' International Association) to which they were affiliated. Similar schemes operated in several other towns and cities, run by artists of the A.I.A. in Oxford, Leamington and Coventry. Requests poured in from many different venues though in one case the proposed designs for wall paintings were rejected because an industrial scene offered for a popular British Restaurant was thought to be unsuitable as 'lacking in sufficient gaiety!'

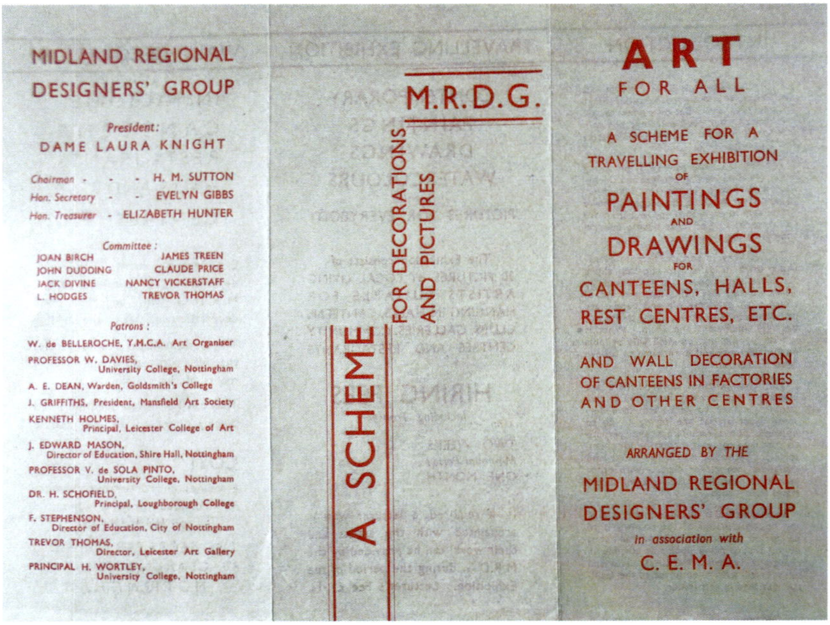

'Art for All' leaflet – Midland Regional Designers' Group 1944

At the group's regular meetings notes were kept on their activities and it is recorded that Murals were requested and painted in a variety of places around Nottingham. Derby's YMCA had several, one of which was photographed for an article by the journalist Nesta Roberts which appeared in 1946 in the September issue of '*Our Time.*' A Nottingham Education Officer asked for murals to be painted at the Boys' Approved School at Risley in 1945 and the same year RAF Syerstone commissioned two for their Officers' Mess. Two further requests came at the end of the war, one for the Miners' Welfare at Teversal and finally, the only one to survive, came Father Marshall's request for a mural of the 'Annunciation' for the small medieval church of St. Martin of Tours. These were both completed, as were the others, and recorded in the group's Minutes book.

Newspapers of the day were keen to report on the unusual and lively activities of this group of artists suddenly arisen in their midst. Evelyn Gibbs attracted much attention as the founder and prime mover of the group and she was also a successful publicist for their various projects. Articles appeared in the Nottingham press about the daring and, some felt, disturbing modernity of paintings shown in their first exhibition, *'Art for All'* held in a city centre department store in August 1943. This exhibition derived from an AIA exhibition held in London earlier the same year, with work by a number of well-known artists. This was supplemented by contributions from the midland artists, and included crafts from local schools and photography from members of a local group. Nottingham newspapers gave extensive coverage of this singular event and continued reporting on the activities of the group.

In autumn 1946 the Nottingham Journal held a report, with a photograph of the progress on the St. Martin's murals. Evelyn Gibbs is shown with Claude Price (a member of the group) on scaffolding in the act of painting the right section of the 'Annunciation' depicting the Angel Gabriel, kneeling as he delivers God's message to Mary. The group's Minutes confirm that the mural had been finished by the date of their meeting on November 8th. Photographs were taken on its completion by a former A.R.P. photographer. These show the entire mural on two sides of the east window, with the altar below, and they remained in the possession of the artist, Evelyn Gibbs. The present writer found them in her studio together with an extensive collection of documents, diaries and personal material when researching the artist's life. It is as a result of having access to this material that it has been possible to piece together the information and circumstances around the commissioning and painting of these murals.

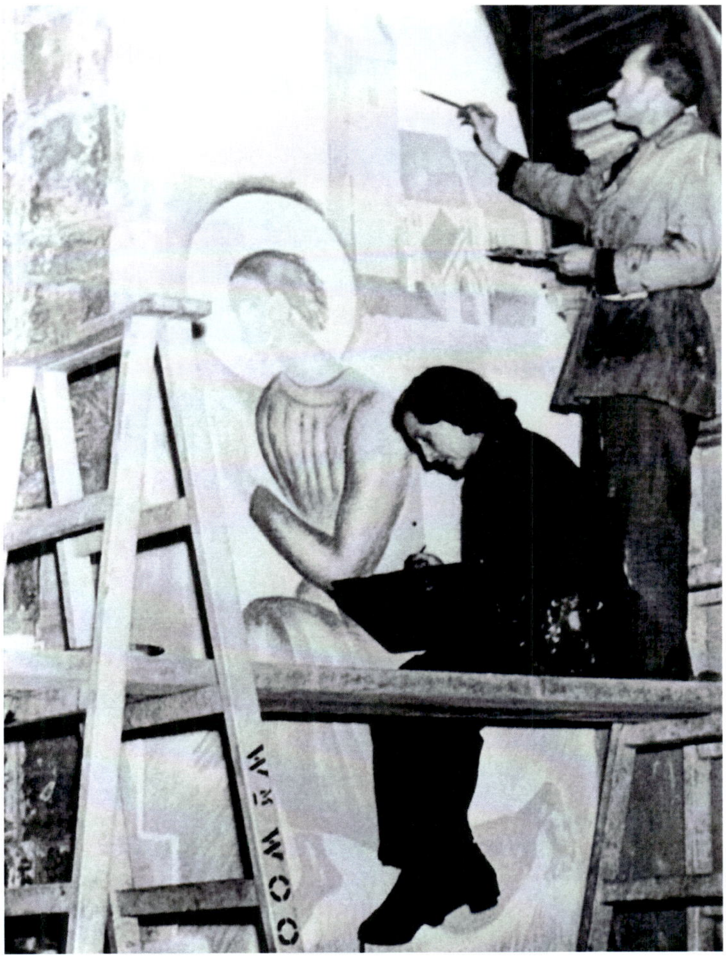

'Painting Murals at Bilborough' Evelyn Gibbs assisted by Claude Price, Nottingham Guardian Journal November 1946

VI ARTISTS AT WORK

The process followed by the Midland Group of artists, as recorded in Minutes of their meetings, entailed notification of all artist members when a commission for a mural, or wall decoration, was received and details then given of scale and other specifications. Artists had to present their designs for consideration by those at the venue. Once a design was selected, other artists could offer help in its painting. Most of the artists active in the group played a part in the various murals executed between 1944 and 1946. It was minuted that Evelyn's design had been selected. Evelyn herself was involved in work on other murals but only the St. Martin's mural was her own design and required something of her former experience in Italy where she studied the great Renaissance frescoes during her scholarship in Rome. She would have seen Fra Angelico's 15th century 'Annunciation' in the Monastery of San Marco, Florence, painted in the true 'buon fresco' manner where the pigment is painted directly into wet lime plaster, bonding the two together. Its design is elegant and unfussy with Mary and the Angel Gabriel shown under a classical portico with a garden just visible beyond, representing a typical 15th century Florentine building. Later murals were often painted onto dry plaster and used egg tempera or later still oil paints.

In the case of the Gibbs mural, although not traditional fresco, she certainly used water based pigments and a lime plaster ground applied beneath. Gibbs might very well have seen another 15th century 'Annunciation' hanging in the National Gallery, Carlo Crivelli's altar piece, probably painted in tempera on wood panel. It is interesting to compare these two works, one so simple and modest, the other rich in detail and complex in story but having again a contemporary background. This was indeed the tradition in so much art of Renaissance Italy, where the religious story was given a local relevance through portraying recognisable topography in the background.

When Evelyn Gibbs embarked on the project she took the traditional approach in basing her image on the Bilborough locality, making St. Martin's church itself the background on the right hand side for the Angel Gabriel's genuflecting figure. Then on the left, the Virgin Mary kneels in front of village buildings which must represent the farm, standing today and used as a community centre. The perspective used here suggests a high view point. It is as though the angel and Mary have dropped down from the heavens to this landscape. This almost cubist effect is cleverly employed to help the formal aspects of design. The key figures, the only ones shown, have a modernity about them, reminiscent of Stanley Spencer's religious paintings. Mary and Gabriel are given haloes but there are no wings for this shaggy-haired Gabriel, unusually placed on the right side of the action. Colouring is mostly in the earth range of pigments, the angel's long robe a warm terracotta set against a background of ochres and soft greens,* while Mary is dressed in a simple blue garment and unadorned, with hands loosely together making the form of a heart shape, behind her the warm tones of farm buildings. They

* Here I have the advantage of the restored paintings.

are the story, larger than life-size and timeless, conveying a great sense of dignity in the way they are posed: the humble attitude of Mary, head bowed, in her recognisable village setting, aware of the grand angel's message, emanating, it seems, from this small local church, bringing together the local and the universal. An art historian, referring to Crivelli's 'Annunciation, with Saint Emidius,' remarked that *'Buildings can lead the eye to another time and emotion, making the unimaginable seem real.'* Father Marshall at Bilborough must have hoped that this image of prophesy, foretelling the birth of Christ, could inspire his congregation with a sense of hope and renewal after the devastation of war.

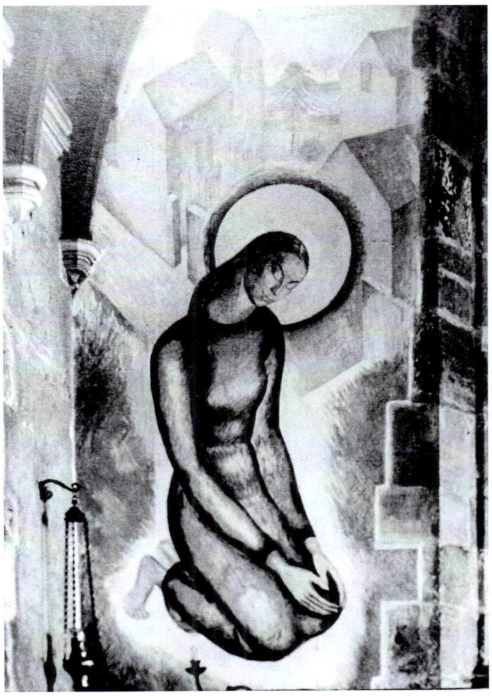

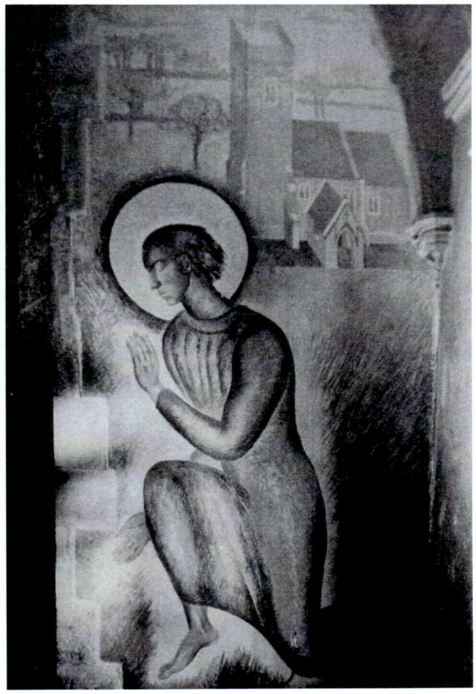

Mural (above left) showing the Virgin Mary with village buildings behind and (above right) Angel Gabriel with St. Martin's church behind – original photographs taken 1946; 'The Graveside' (below left) engraving, 1928;'The West Garden' (below right) etching, Rome 1931

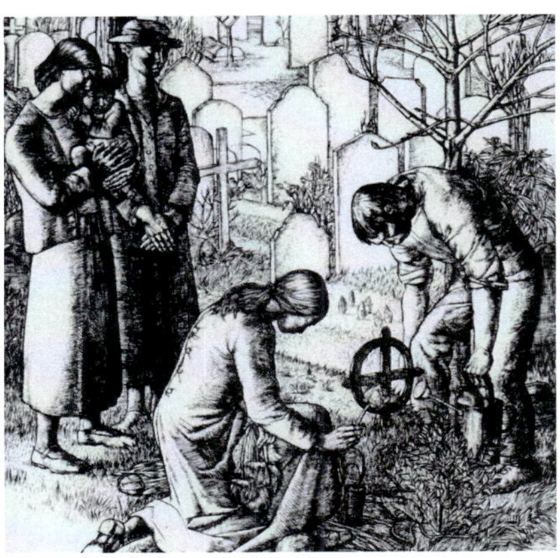

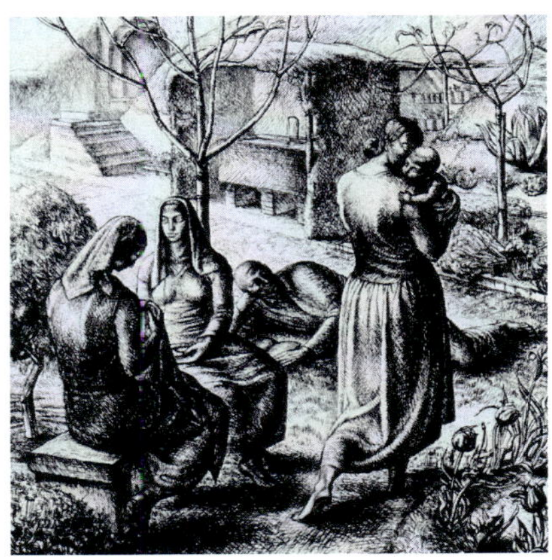

VII LIVERPOOL, LONDON, ROME AND ART TEACHING

Reference has been made earlier to Evelyn Gibbs' training and her career as artist and educationist but some examination of the decades prior to her arrival in Nottingham will help us understand what shaped her achievements. Her initial training at the City School of Art in Liverpool emphasised graphic accomplishments, in drawing, composition and illustration leading to her scholarship to the Royal College of Arts in London to enrol in the School of Etching and Engraving in 1926. She had already made several etchings at Liverpool of local subjects such as 'The New Brighton Ferry' inspired by her father's occupation as a Marine Engineer working in the Merchant Navy. The dockland area would have been particularly fascinating for his daughter. In London she joined Catherine Deane, a friend and former student from Liverpool, with whom she shared digs, and where they were joined by Elisabeth Vellacott, a painting student. All three remained great friends throughout their lives. Whilst at the R.C.A. Evelyn Gibbs worked on her etchings and engravings, while also making drawings from life models in college studios. In her own time she would sketch landscapes and make portraits of her friends.

All this was to be of immense value in her future artistic career. Etching is a notoriously difficult skill to learn but Gibbs excelled and after three years studying under her tutor, Malcom Osborne, she applied for an extra scholarship, the Prix de Rome, offering particular prints for assessment. Her success gave her the Scholarship in Etching and Engraving for 1929 –31. One of her prize winning prints was 'The Graveside' an engraving of great delicacy with sensitively drawn grieving figures, showing a highly developed personal style of figure drawing, recognisable in much of her later work. Gibbs' printmaking in Rome included many compositions where figures were set in a landscape, such as 'Morning' and 'Trattoria,' both the result of careful preparatory drawings of individual figures and of landscape studies. This was the way she worked and would always work. First the drawings or sketches then would follow the finished work as etching or engraving or, later, in her many paintings. The emphasis on line which is crucial in these forms of printing becomes part of her style generally and can be seen in most of her mature painting. There is a very linear style of painting to be seen, for instance in her 'Annunciation' mural where brushstrokes are like the hatching lines found in drawing and etching.

The years in Rome were exhilarating and rewarding, artistically. They should have set Gibbs on a successful career path in printmaking and illustration but the Wall Street Crash and depression years to follow in the 1930s destroyed those hopes for her and many others. Instead, Evelyn Gibbs decided to apply for teaching positions in London schools. This was a new venture for her and a time of great activity in the field of Art Education, where advanced theories were moving away from the older practices, becoming more based on the imagination of children than on the coercive styles previously used. Influenced by the Modern movement in 20th century art, artists and art historians admired the innocent art of children and the craft inspired art of non-western civilisations. Paul Klee, Gauguin, Picasso and others had shown in their work a new delight and vigour derived from these sources.

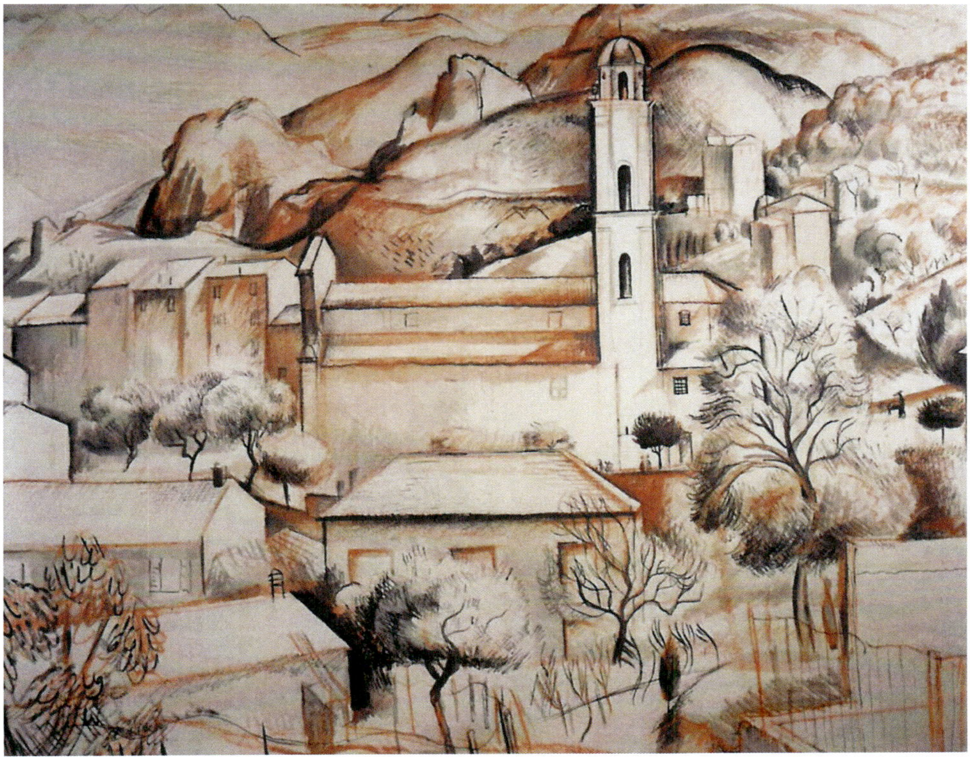

'Piana Corsica', ink and conté, 1937 (above); 'Bomb Damage', drawing, 1941 (below)

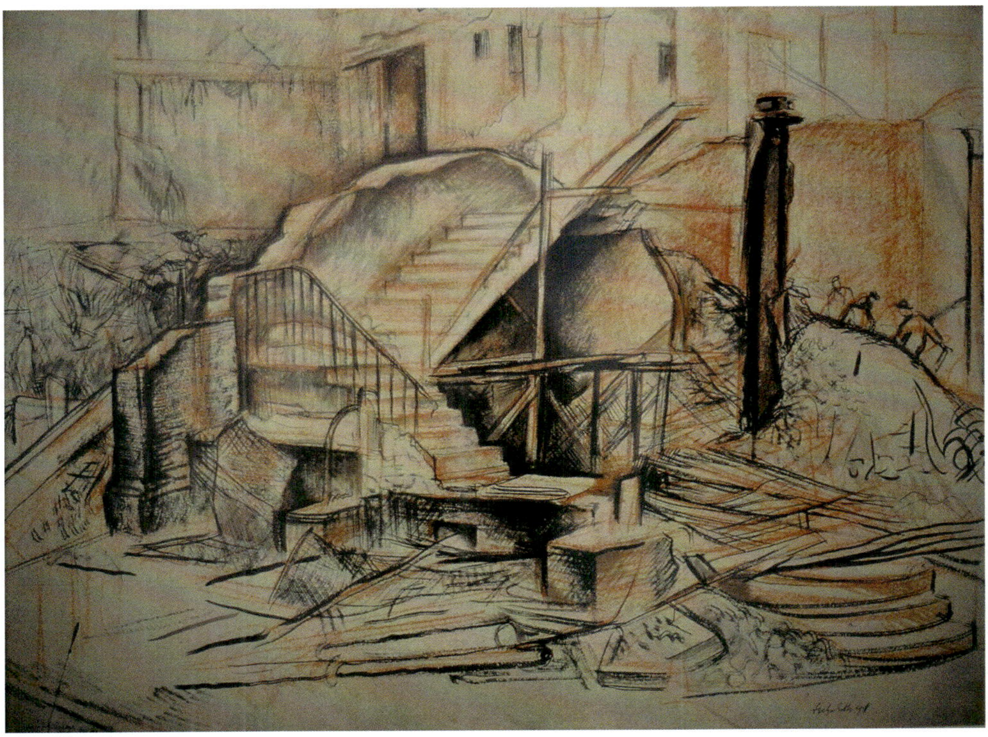

Gibbs began to contribute to the current art journals, writing a series of articles on Imaginative Painting and craft skills for teachers to use. This led to calls for her to write a book based on these articles with examples of children's art from her own classes. '*The Teaching of Art in Schools…*' by Evelyn Gibbs, published in 1934 has a Foreward by Edwin Glasgow, Keeper of the National Gallery. It was received with rapturous reviews. One in *The Listener* puts 'Here are set forth with such liveliness and conviction the occupations suitable for children – the making of large paintings, strong in colour and vigorous in brushwork, the simple crafts of linocutting… a first in its particular field.' Its success led to the offer of a lectureship at Goldsmiths' College in London where she could take her ideas directly to the teaching profession.

In her own art she had less time to make prints but continued to draw and paint, exhibiting with various art societies including the Women's International Art Club. She produced some large finely drawn landscapes in ink, and conté in France and Corsica on her holiday visits in the late 1930s. Most important for what was to follow was her membership of the A.I.A., which demonstrated against the rise of Fascism through exhibitions, meetings and the support given to refugee artists. These exhibitions became a roll call of the younger up and coming artists, including Henry Moore, John Piper, Betty Rea and Nan Youngman, as well as older established artists and art critics. Gibbs would remain in touch with many of these artists after her move to Nottingham, inviting them to exhibit and talk about their work.

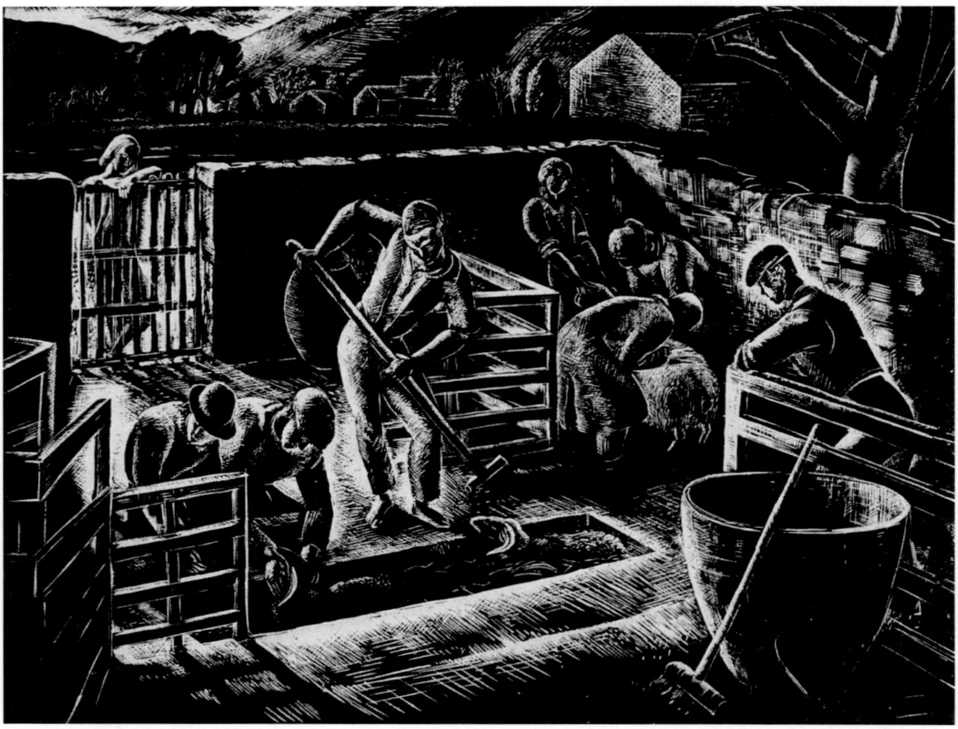

'Sheep Shearing in Yorkshire' wood engraving 1937

VIII NOTTINGHAM

During the war and for some years afterwards, Evelyn Gibbs lived at a house on Clarendon Street, Nottingham, which belonged to Hugh Willatt, a solicitor working in his family's law firm. They had met soon after Gibbs arrived when she joined the Cooperative Arts theatre and offered her help devising sets for their plays. Hugh Willatt directed many of their productions and soon they became closely involved and planned to marry after his war service in the RAF had finished. This brought about a major change in Gibbs' life. She had the use of this house as home, studio and meeting venue for her increasingly active artists' group, from its inception in 1943. Several of her paintings are recognisable as views looking out into the street from the house. One shows a snowy street with houses on the opposite side near a cemetery. Others developed from drawings made all over the city but particularly from the high vantage point of the Castle pathways, looking down across houses, railyards and beyond through quantities of smoke and steam. 'Smoking Chimneys' is aptly named, showing a city sheathed in smoke from industrial and domestic sources. Nottingham was bombed in the early years of war and many lives were disrupted by loss and bereavement. Like other cities devastation was all around when Gibbs recorded war damage in two impressive mixed media drawings, both titled 'Bomb Damage'. They are among a series of works made in Nottingham, recording the scenes around her in wartime.

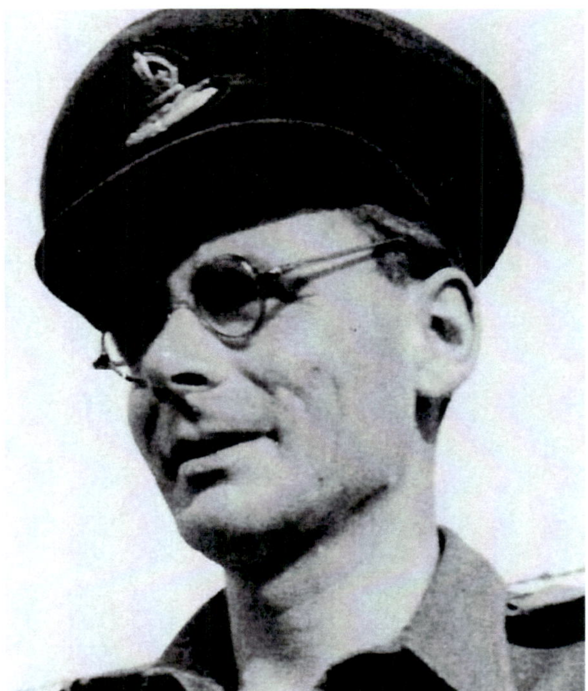

Hugh Willatt, c1943

IX POST WAR NOTTINGHAM

Hugh Willatt returned from his war service in the Middle East in 1945 and the couple married later that year. As part of her new life and possibly because of regulations for the employment of married women, Gibbs gave up her full time teaching at Goldsmiths' for a less demanding timetable but continued her WEA classes at the Adult Education Centre, on Shakespeare Street. She took on new roles as Art Advisor to the Education committees of Nottinghamshire, Derbyshire and Leicestershire Councils. This meant she was involved in selecting contemporary artworks for circulating to schools through the inspired "Pictures for Schools" enterprise in post-war England and Wales.

A photograph shows her at work in her new studio on the top, attic floor of a building on the corner of Houndsgate. She is painting the street scene below with a view of buildings opposite as she looked across the road to a Shipstones pub (no longer there) near St. Peter's church. This is 'Nottingham Window', now in the collection of Nottingham Castle Museum with a number of her other paintings, drawings and prints.

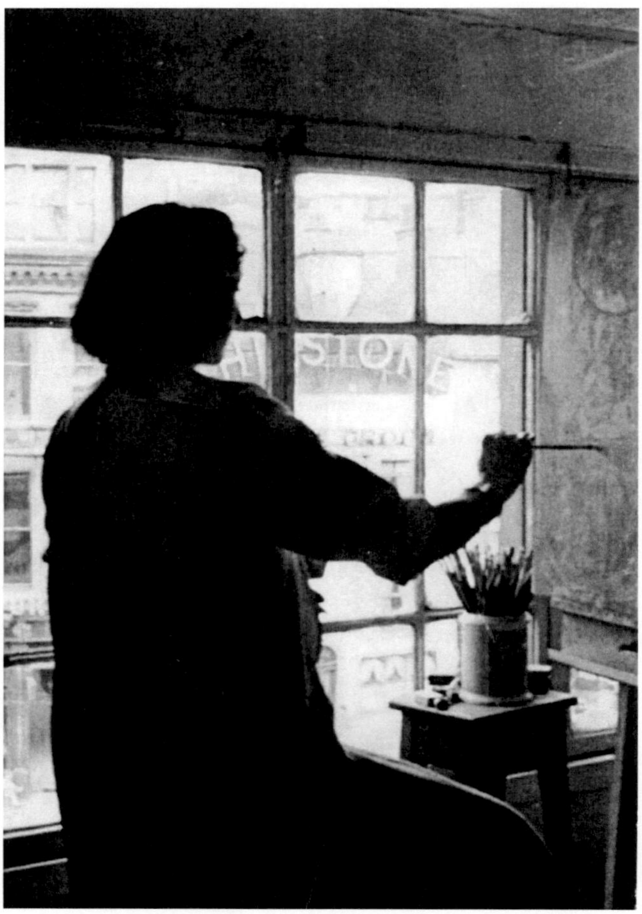

Evelyn Gibbs at her studio window, Houndsgate Nottingham, c1947

It is likely that Gibbs had begun to use this studio in 1946 when she started her work on the St. Martin's mural of the Annunciation. She had, in effect, to consider two paintings, occupying the high walls on either side of the stained glass window. On visits to the church she will have made drawings of the buildings nearby to see how they might fit with her overall design and she must also have considered the height and surface of the walls she was required to cover. Minutes record that time was taken preparing the walls with smooth plaster in readiness for painting. Once dry there needed to be applications of a lime plaster ground to lie directly under the mural. The floor of her studio would allow her to lay out the nearly twelve foot scaled-up drawings or cartoons of the two designs, which she then had to 'square up' for transferring, section by section to the church walls, which had been prepared the same way.

Relieved no doubt to have satisfactorily completed this huge double mural, Evelyn Gibbs had time for easel painting once more. She had commissions for portraits and made many paintings of friends and their children. Her friend Elizabeth Barnard, music specialist at Goldsmiths', met and married Manuel Lazareno, a Spanish refugee musician,

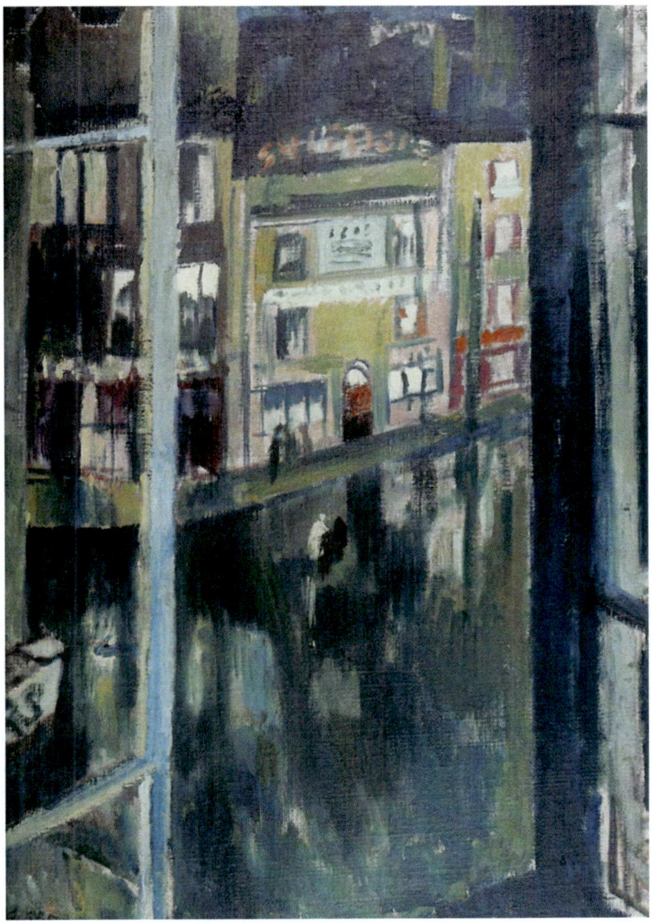

'Nottingham Window', oils on canvas, 1948, Nottingham City Museums and Galleries

whose portrait Gibbs painted and gave to her friend while in Nottingham. There are two delightful portraits of the young daughter of Arthur Ledger, also named Evelyn, holding one of the artist's cats. Theatrical subjects were on hand through Hugh Willatt's important role in Nottingham's theatre world. Gibbs made drawings and paintings of actors, often in costume. When Chekhov's *The Seagull* was performed at the Playhouse, Gibbs drew Carol Marsh as Nina holding the form of a dead seagull. Requests for Illustration work came from Nottingham writer Hilda Lewis who asked for cover designs and illustrations for several of her novels, including *The Ship that Flew, The Gentle Falcon, The Witch and the Priest.*

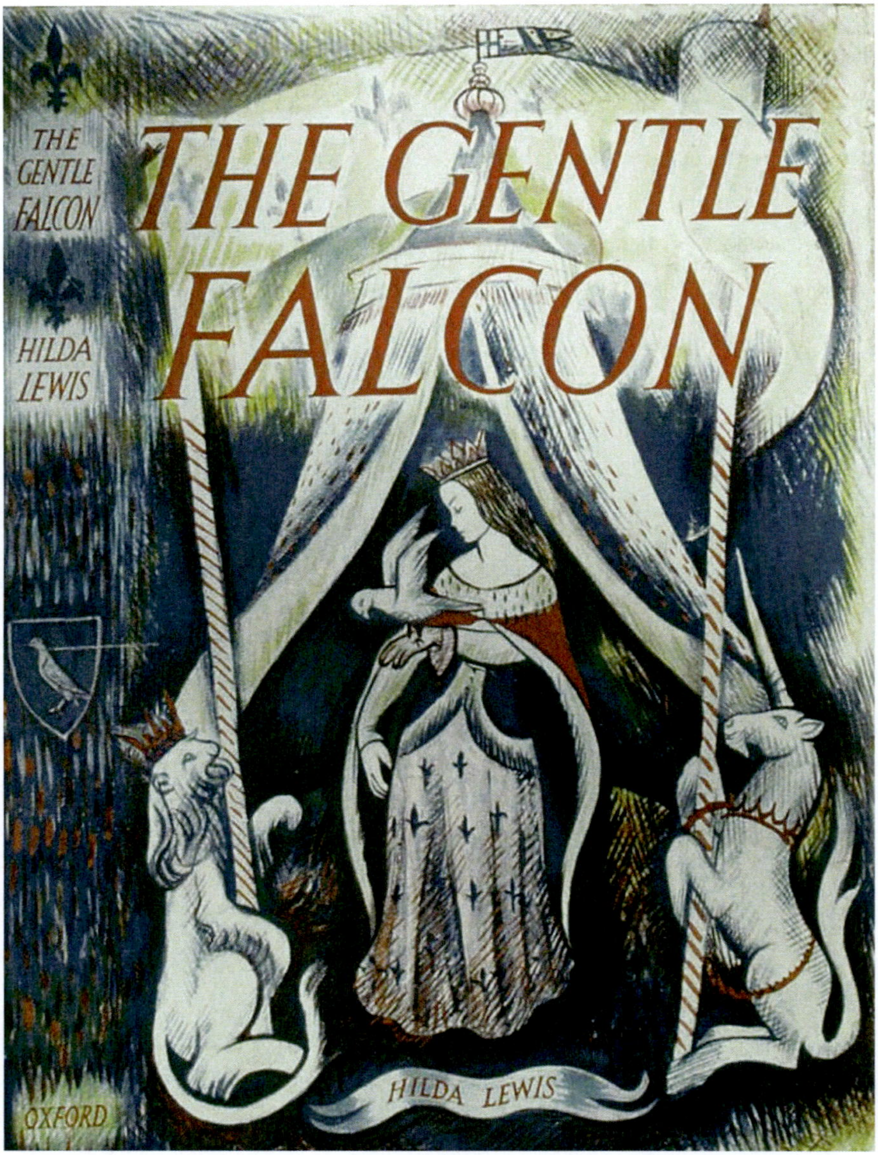

'The Gentle Falcon' by Hilda Lewis, cover design and illustrations, OUP 1952

X POST WAR TRAVELS

Like many artists of her time, Gibbs was keen to travel abroad again after the war and made painting trips to Ireland, then further afield to France, Spain and Italy, returning with material for her regular exhibitions in Nottingham and London galleries. 'Grape Harvest', painted in the early 1950s, is amongst many lively oil paintings showing the harvesting of crops or the work of fishermen and women unravelling their nets. Happy

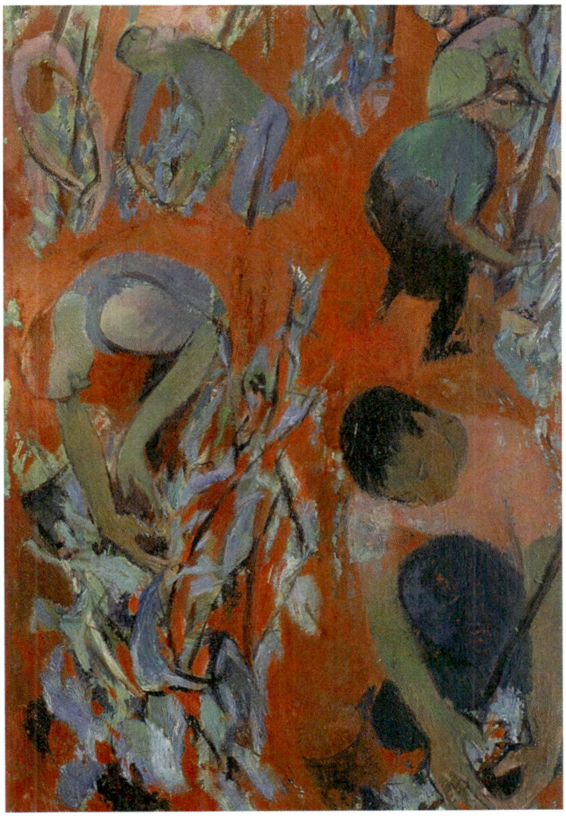

'Grape Harvest' oils on canvas, 1950s

and busy years for both Evelyn Gibbs and Hugh Willatt during a time when Britain was extending its patronage of the Arts, through the post war creation of the Arts Council. Willatt gave much of his time to the Council while Gibbs, continuing her role as Honorary Secretary of the Midland Group, applied for funds to keep local galleries afloat. The Midland Group had been able to move from small first floor premises to larger and more impressive buildings, whilst still running as a voluntary body.

By 1960 when Gibbs and Willatt moved to London, plans were afoot for the Midland Group to take premises at Wellington Circus and for the new Playhouse theatre, designed by Peter Moro, to open across the road, due in no small manner to Hugh Willatt's advocacy.

XI LONDON AND BEYOND

On moving to London, Evelyn Gibbs was able to return to her first love, printmaking. She now had her own printing press, passed on from her Royal College tutor Malcom Osborne. The new prints were considerably larger than her former student ones and involved an increasing use of aquatint and deep bite etching. There were landscape based works, from drawings of rocks made in Anglesey with her old friend Beth Vellacott and figure-based etchings such as 'Georgie of Paddington,' where she made adventurous use of texture in the background of this striking study of a young boy. When Gibbs accompanied her husband, now chairing an Arts Council panel, on a visit to Persia (Iran today), she made drawings of veiled Muslim women, which inspired a series of fine etchings. There were paintings too but it was evident that Gibbs was engrossed in more avant garde experiments, following William Hayter's influential abstract prints and those of Julian Trevelyan. She exhibited her new prints at the latest Midland Group gallery in 1965 at which she was photographed displaying her copper etching plate in front of the resulting etching.

In 1972 Hugh Willatt received a knighthood in recognition of his work as Secretary General of the Arts Council after many years of devoted service. He was widely admired for his warmth and enthusiasm, a great believer in the 'arms-length' principle, allowing creative inspiration to flourish in the arts. Throughout his life, he gave his wife unlimited support and continued to foster the long- term preservation of her reputation, aiding and encouraging

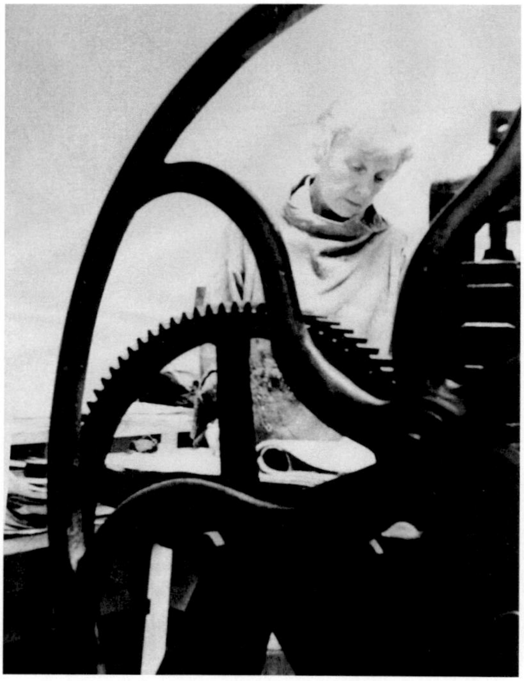

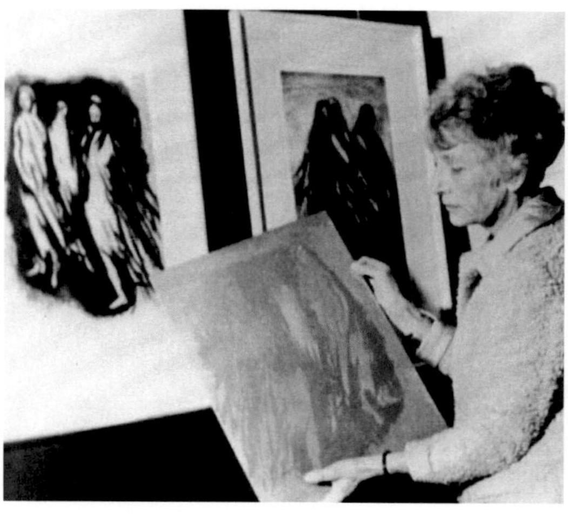

Top: Gibbs at her etching press 1965.
Bottom: Evelyn Gibbs at her Midland Group exhibition in 1965.

retrospective exhibitions until his own death in 1996. Evelyn Gibbs retained her own name as artist but was occasionally named Lady Willatt.

From the late 1960s the couple had explored the Maltese island of Gozo, buying and restoring an old house which became almost a second home for Gibbs. She was entranced by the bare rocky landscapes where saltpans formed extraordinary shapes in the rocks near the sea, creating an almost lunar landscape, as revealed in her haunting late works. Rock forms had fascinated her for years and she made numerous drawings of these elemental structures, later to become paintings and large coloured etchings, increasingly abstract in appearance. In 1976 Curwen Press commissioned a set of lithographs of the Thames at Hammersmith, near their London home, and of views of Gozo. The following year a major exhibition of these was held in Valletta and much of this exhibition also travelled to London and to Nottingham for viewing at the University's gallery. But for Gibbs, work had become more difficult with the onset of Parkinsons' Disease, despite the unwavering support of her husband. Even when she became dependent on a wheelchair, they still travelled back to their beloved Gozo. Drawing was still possible into the 1980s until a stroke prevented further work. Evelyn Gibbs died on 27th February 1991.

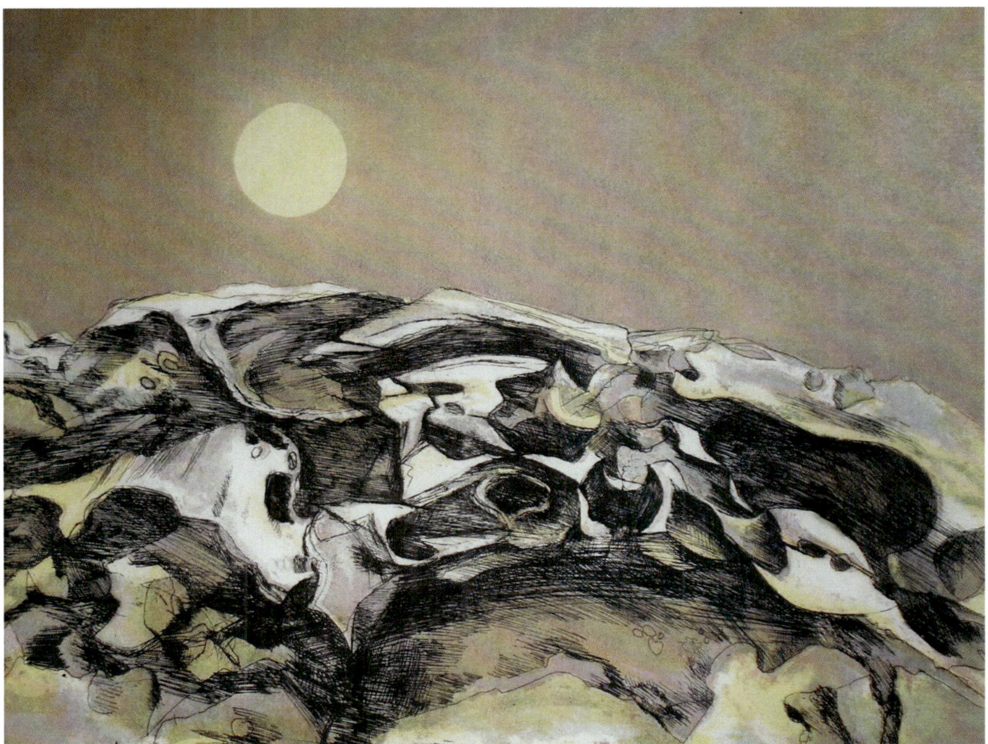

'Sunset Dwerja' etching with aquatint, 1974

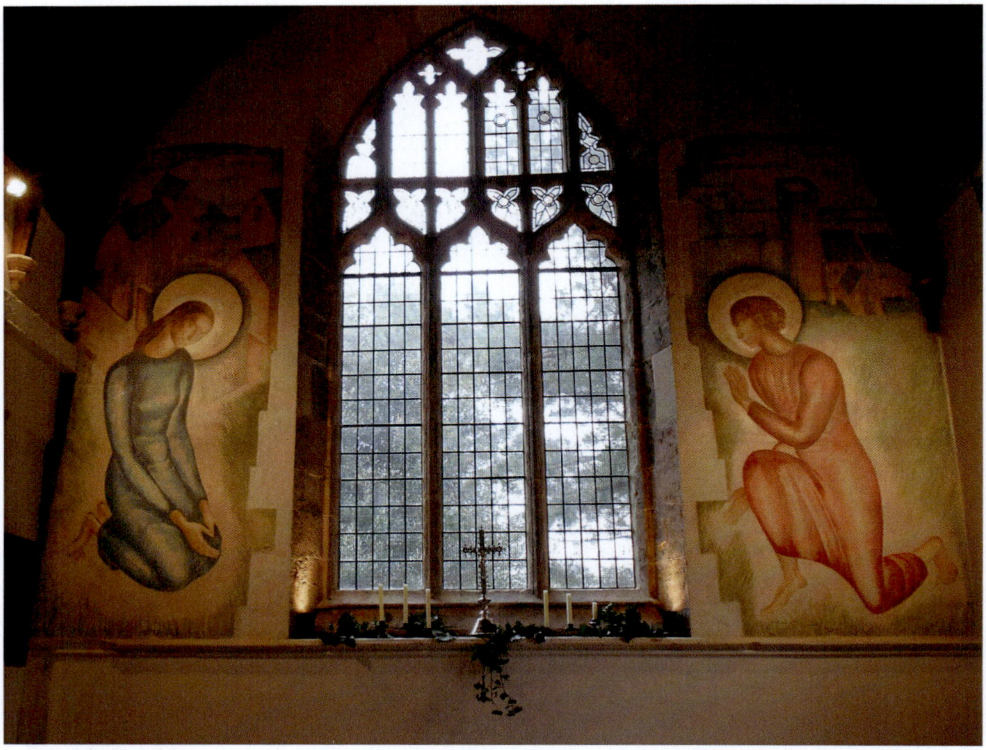

The completed restoration of the 'Annunciation' mural in November 2014

XII CONSERVATION AND RESTORATION

In conclusion, there is the exciting story to tell of the successful reappearance of Evelyn Gibbs' mural of the 'Annunciation' in November 2014, sixty eight years after its completion and some forty since it was obscured in the 1970s. A combination of factors came together in 2009 when electricians showed photographs of visible, but graffitied, paintings hidden above the chancel ceiling. The Reverend Amanda Cartwright had recently been appointed vicar of St. Martin's and two nearbye parishes but the churchwarden, Hilary Wheat, remembered these paintings from childhood. Soon they contacted the biographer of Evelyn Gibbs. The next stage was to consult English Heritage who advised that a condition survey should be made by expert conservation specialist, Tobit Curteis. An exceedingly thorough examination of the walls and paintwork resulted in the recommendation that restoration was indeed possible if funds could be found. Much work was then needed in fundraising for the repairs of the entire church, which would need to take place before any restoration work on the murals. For such extensive building and conservation work to be carried out, the Heritage Lottery Fund was approached and applications were made for the initial grant to establish costs. By now a committee had been formed by Hilary Wheat, comprising Rev. Amanda Cartwright, Simon Gledhill, Bruce Bradley and myself. In September 2012 the project was awarded a Stage 1. Development grant. This enabled Bruce Bradley, the architect, to begin work on detailed plans for the reconstruction of the church and to discuss them with possible contractors. Bit by bit over many meetings, fundraising events and publicity exercises, following HLF guidelines, the next stage was reached in late 2013. At last the Stage 2 grant was agreed, giving permission for conservation quality restoration work to begin in 2014.

In April of that year building work commenced with the arrival of specialist, heritage conservation teams of builders and stone masons, including trainee apprentices from the local community. They completed the extensive restoration of the church by mid September after which the painting conservation team, led by Tobit Curteis, could begin their restoration of the newly exposed murals. Just as Evelyn Gibbs had painted from scaffolding in 1946, Bianca and Claudia, now stood or crouched on scaffolding in front of the original painting, as they worked to clean and conserve any damaged areas. Joy and Saskia came next to restore, by repainting, the lower sections hidden beneath emulsion paint. All this was most excellently achieved and the beautiful church was reunited with its wonderful murals in November 2014.

Many people deserve acknowledgment for their part in this thrilling and successful enterprise. Very great thanks are due to individuals in English Heritage and the Heritage Lottery Fund who have been on hand throughout to advise and safeguard the project but the hard work was done by stone masons, builders, glaziers and the painting conservation team led by Tobit Curteis.

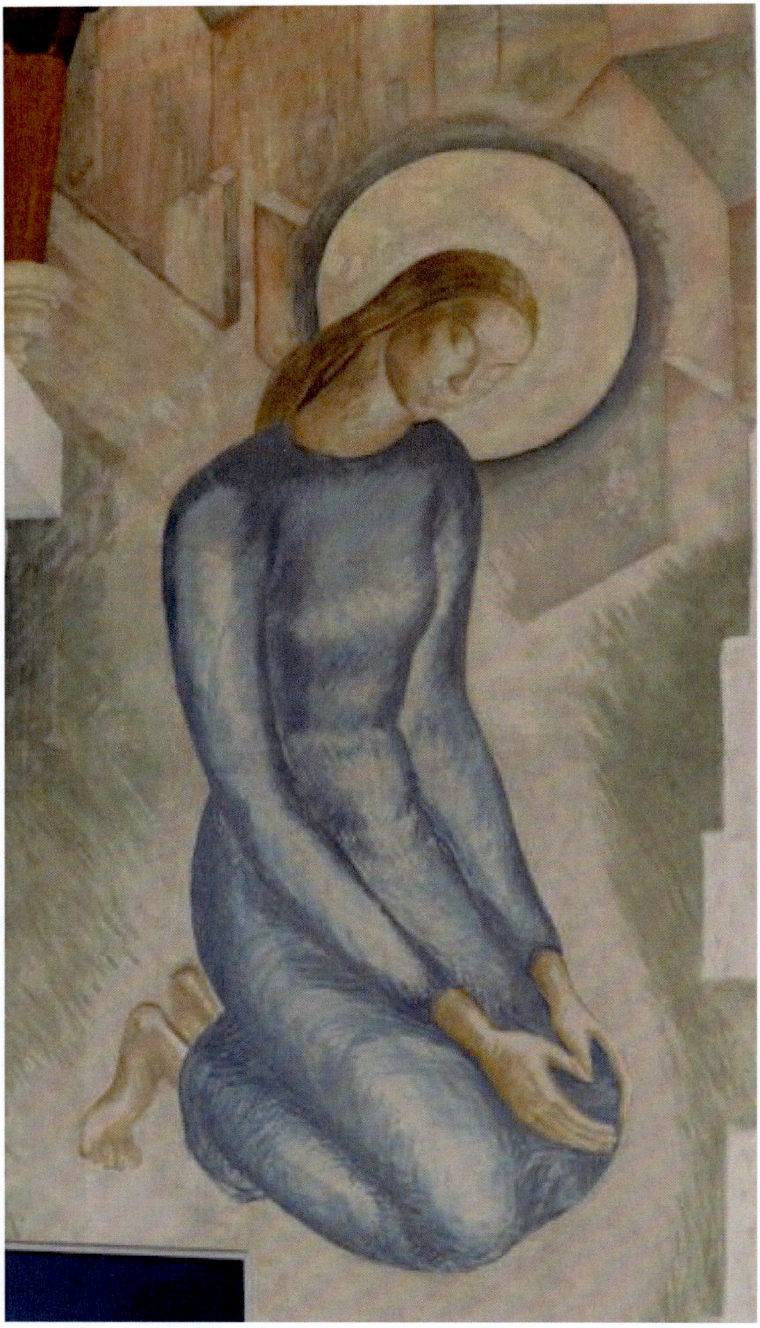

Restored mural showing the Virgin Mary with village buildings, November 2014
photo by Tobit Curteis

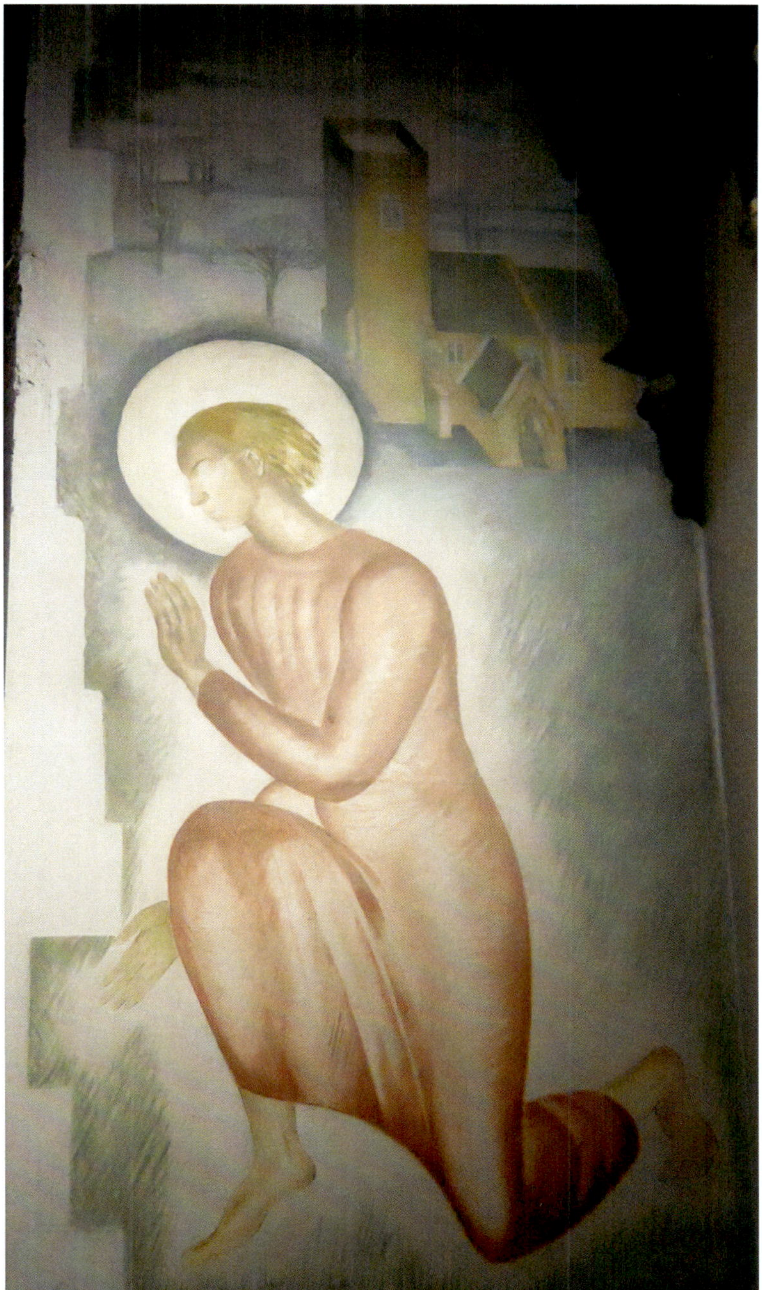

Restored mural showing Angel Gabriel with St. Martin's church behind, November 2014
photo by Hilary Wheat

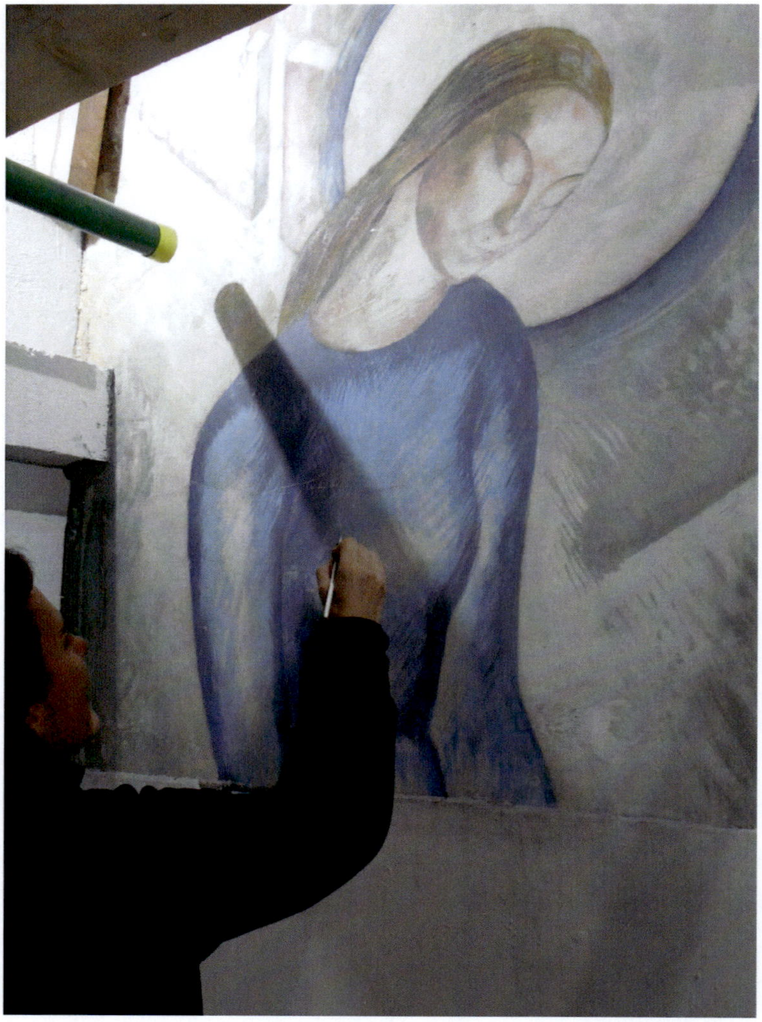

Conservation work in progress with C.F., October 2014, photo by Pauline Lucas

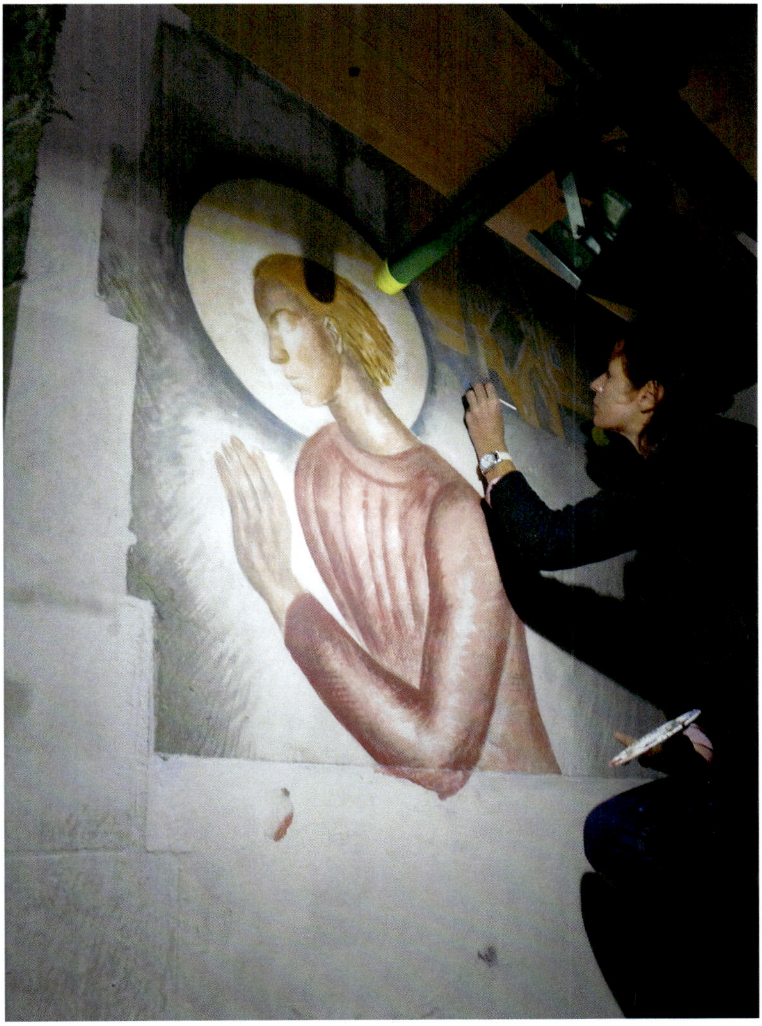

Conservation work in progress with B.M., October 2014, photo by Pauline Lucas

The following pages list the key events and dates in the life of Evelyn Gibbs forming a Chronology

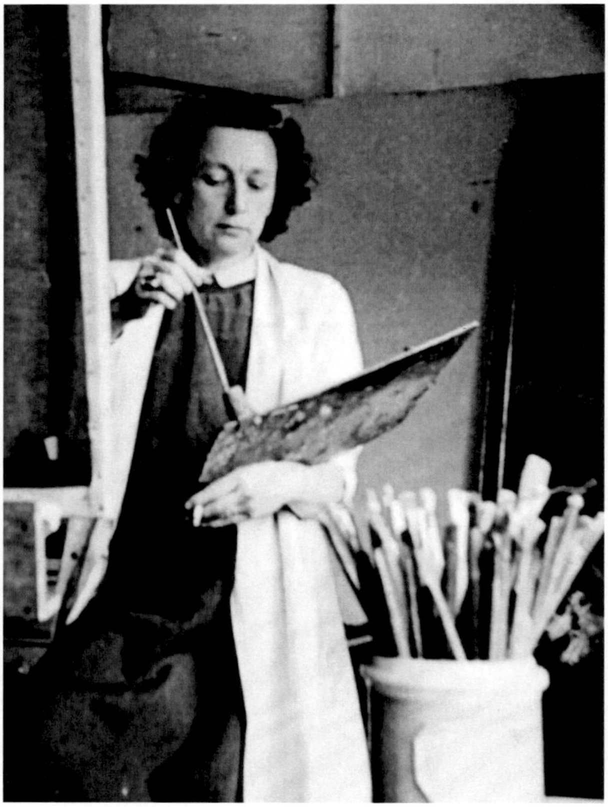

Evelyn Gibbs painting in her studio c1947

EVELYN GIBBS CHRONOLOGY

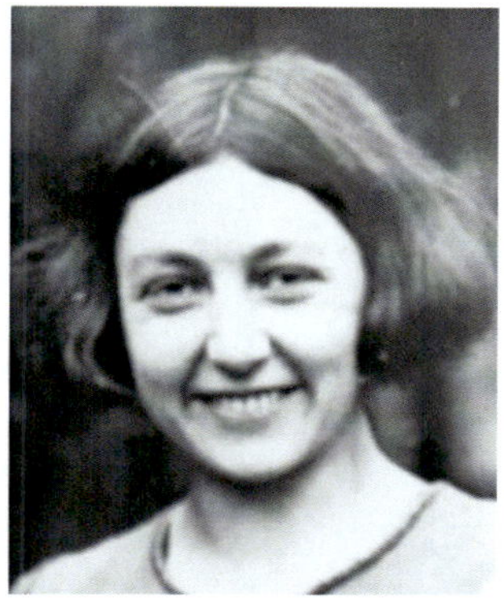

Evelyn Gibbs as a student

1905 May 3, Evelyn May Gibbs born in Liverpool
Mother, Euphemia, pianist and singer
Father, Horace, Marine Engineer

1907 Sister, Molly, born

1912 Brother, Lawrence, born

1922 Enters Liverpool School of Art

1926 Wins Scholarship to the Royal School of Art, London, School of Engraving
Friendships with Catherine Deane and Elisabeth Vellacott

1929 Wins 'Prix de Rome' in Engraving
Working 2 years at British School at Rome

1931 Returns to Liverpool, then teaching Art in London schools

1934 'The Teaching of Art in Schools' by Evelyn Gibbs, published by Williams & Norgate Ltd
Appointed Lecturer at Goldsmiths' College

1936 Mother dies in Liverpool

1937 Joins A.I.A. (Artists International Association) and W.I.A.C. (Womens International Art Club)
Sketching in France and Corsica

1938 Exhibits in A.I.A. 'Portraits for Spain'

1939 Exhibits in A.I.A. 'Unity of Artists for Peace, Democracy and Cultural Development'
Sketching with Elisabeth Vellacott in France and Corsica
War declared. Gibbs evacuated with Goldsmiths' College to Nottingham

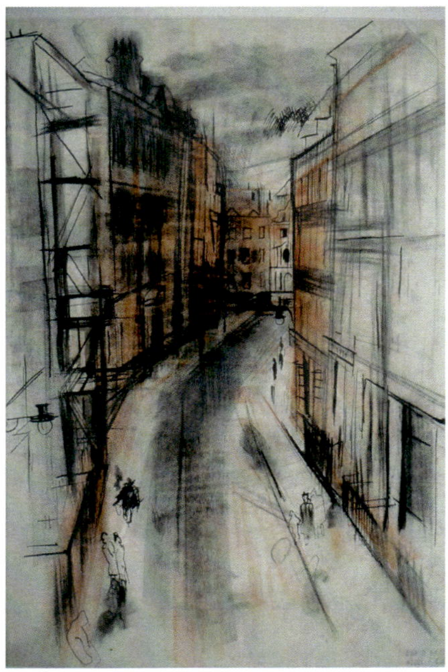

'Nottingham Street' drawing; 1950s

1940-3	Teaching and working with theatre groups where Gibbs meets Hugh Willatt, soon to join RAF in Middle East
1943	Exhibits at A.I.A. 'For Liberty' exhibition at John Lewis, London February 23, first meeting of 'Nottingham Regional Designers Group' affiliated A.I.A. August 14 - 28, 'Art For All' exhibition by Group September, Gibbs commissioned by War Artists Advisory Committee to make drawings at Raleigh Factory, Blood Transfusion units and WVS painting
1944	Second 'Art for All' exhibition Death of Horace Gibbs in Liverpool
1945	May 8, Peace declared – end of War in Europe. Hugh Willatt returns and marries Evelyn Gibbs Midland Regional Designers Group opens first gallery at 20 St. James St.
1946	Gibbs exhibits in London gallery and sketches in Ireland Gibbs design chosen for 'Annunciation' mural at St. Martin's Church Bilborough completed in November Group's murals at Derby, Risley, Teversal and Syerstone
1947	MRDG opens new gallery at 44a Clumber St. with Gibbs exhibition in October
1948-9	Painting in south of France MRDG opens 3rd gallery at 11 Park Row Gibbs advising county councils 'Pictures for Schools' collections

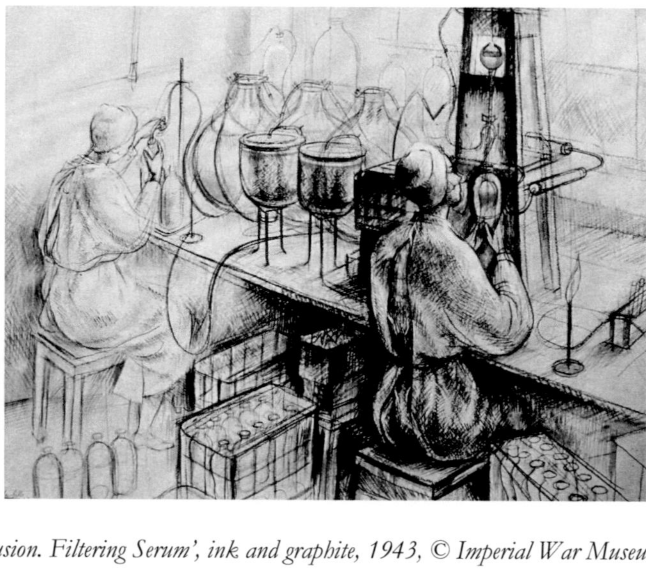

'Blood Transfusion. Filtering Serum', ink and graphite, 1943, © Imperial War Museum (IWM) London

1950-51	Painting in Brittany, south of France and Italy, meeting Mary Fedden in San Gimignano Festival of Britain exhibition 'Our Region' by Midland Group Gibbs solo exhibition at Midland Group and painting in R.A. exhibition
1952	4th gallery opened by Midland Group at 38 Bridlesmith Gate
1953	Gibbs exhibiting at Nottingham Castle and London galleries
1954	Gibbs solo exhibition 'Drawings of France & Corsica' at Zwemmer gallery Sketching in France and Spain
1955	Exhibits in 'Young Midland Artists' at Zwemmers Invited to join BBC Midland Critics
1956-59	Travelling, sketching and painting in Yugoslavia, Italy, France, Spain and Portugal
1957	Exhibits with Sylvia Melland at Zwemmers and with Marion Adnams at Midland Group
1958	15th Anniversary Party for Midland Group

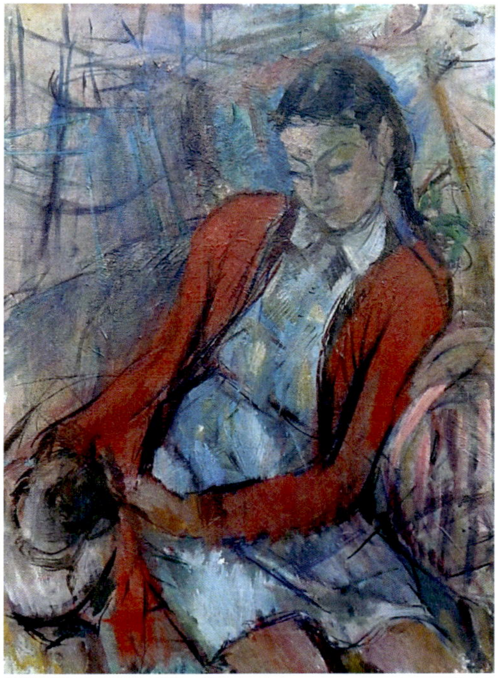

'Girl with Cat', 1949 (above);
Mural in a Derby Canteen M.R.D. group, from 'Artists in the Provinces' by N.M.Roberts, Our Time, 1946 (below)

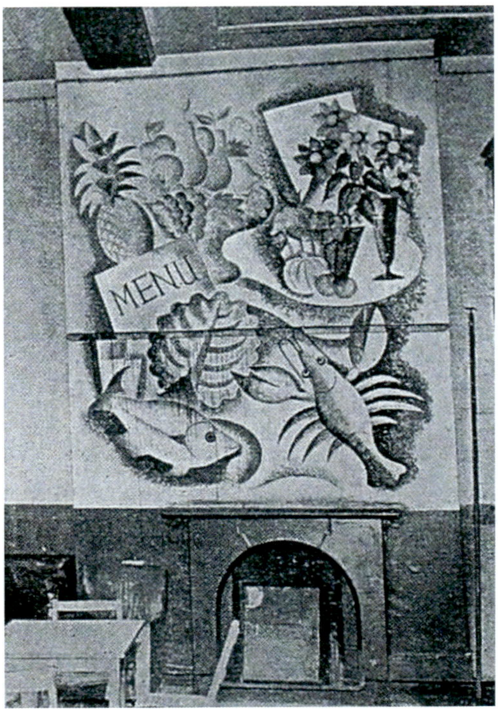

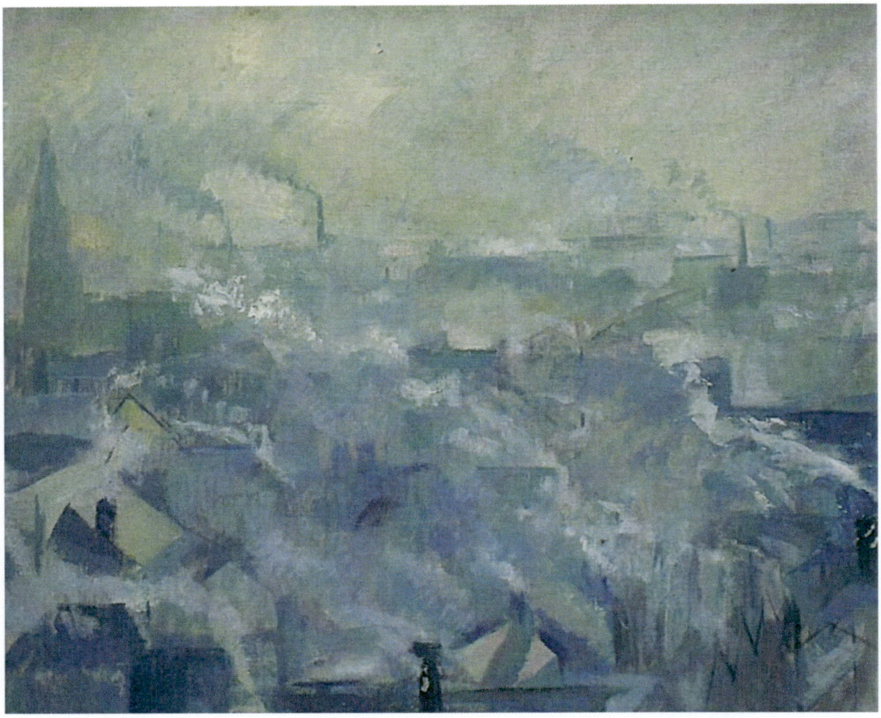

'Smoking Chimneys', oils on canvas, 1951 (above);
'Clarendon Street in Snow', oils on canvas, c1946 (below)

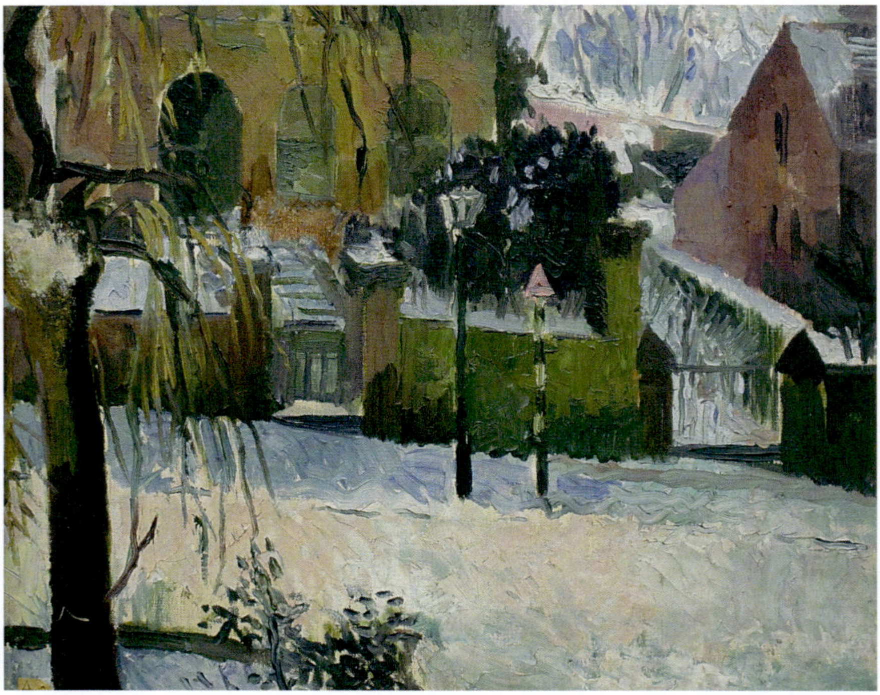

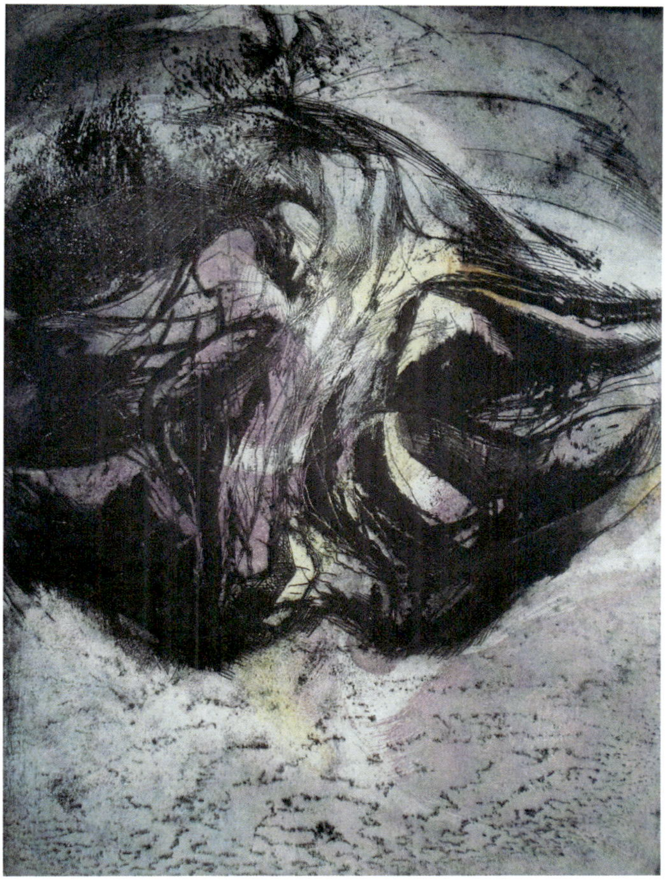

'Lunar Rock' etching and aquatint 1966 (left); 'Sea Rock' etching and aquatint 1965 (below)

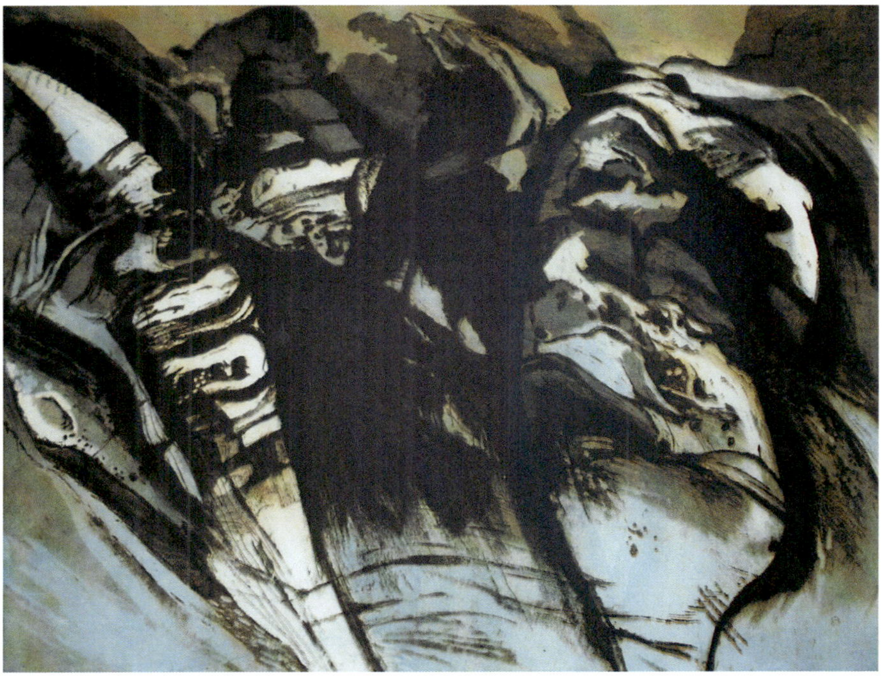

1960	Gibbs and Willatt preparing to leave Nottingham for London as the Midland Group prepares to move to large new premises at East Circus Street, Wellington Circus
1961	Exhibits 'Recent Drawings' at Leicester Galleries Sketching on Anglesey with Elisabeth Vellacott Opening of new Midland Group Gallery
1962	Gibbs exhibition at Midland Group Gallery, 68 drawings and paintings, including rock and sea images from Anglesey Elected President in honour of her past work for the Group
1963	Gibbs exhibition at Ivan Spence Gallery, Ibiza
1964	Gibbs Exhibition at Forum Gallery, Bristol Visits Persia (now Iran) with Hugh Willatt and Ballet Rambert for Arts Council. Many drawings of veiled women form basis for etchings Sketching rocks and sea around Scilly Isles
1965	Exhibits much of this work in 'Recent Etchings and Drawings' at Midland Group Gallery
1966-9	Working on etchings and large oil paintings
1968	Hugh Willatt appointed Secretary General of the Arts Council
1969	Visiting the Maltese Island of Gozo, they buy a farmhouse to renovate Gozo provides endless scope for Gibbs drawing and painting
1970	Gibbs exhibits 'Drawings, Paintings and Etchings' at the Drian Galleries and Nottingham University Gallery

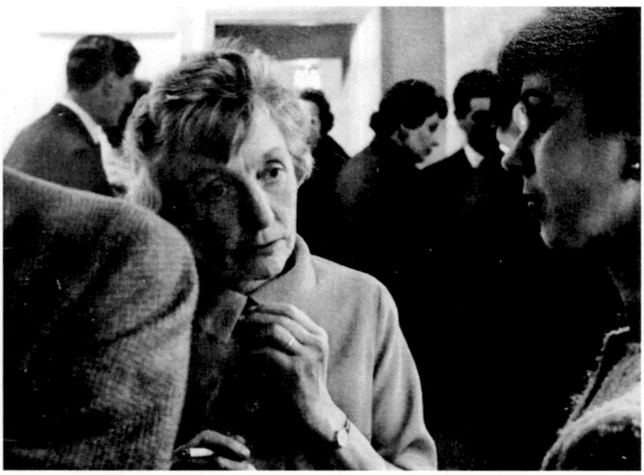

Gibbs and Sylvia Cooper at the Midland Group gallery 1960s

1972 Gibbs exhibits 'Drawings and Etchings' at Drian Galleries
Hugh Willatt knighted for work at Arts Council

1974 They move to Hammersmith Terrace, Trevelyan Trust artists' studios, planned by Julian Trevelyan and Mary Fedden, at Durham Wharf
Gibbs exhibition at Gallery 359, Nottingham

1976 Commissioned by Curwen Press to make lithographs of Gozo and Thames at Hammersmith

1977 Exhibits these at Curwen Gallery
Gibbs exhibition 'Drawings, Etchings and Lithographs' at Museum of Fine Arts, Valletta, Malta. Exhibits at New Art Centre
Experiencing symptoms of Parkinson's Disease

1981 Gibbs diagnosed as suffering from Parkinson's Disease but exhibits 'Six Hammersmith Artists' at Riverside Studios

1984 'Artists under the Flag' war artists at Gillian Jason Gallery
'The Garden of Flora' at Nottingham Castle

1985 Made Fellow of Royal Society of Painter-Etchers and Engravers, R.E.

1988 'Evelyn Gibbs Early Etchings' 1927 – 1930 Garton & Co print dealers
Still visiting Gozo but confined to a wheelchair

1991 February 27, Evelyn Gibbs dies at home in London

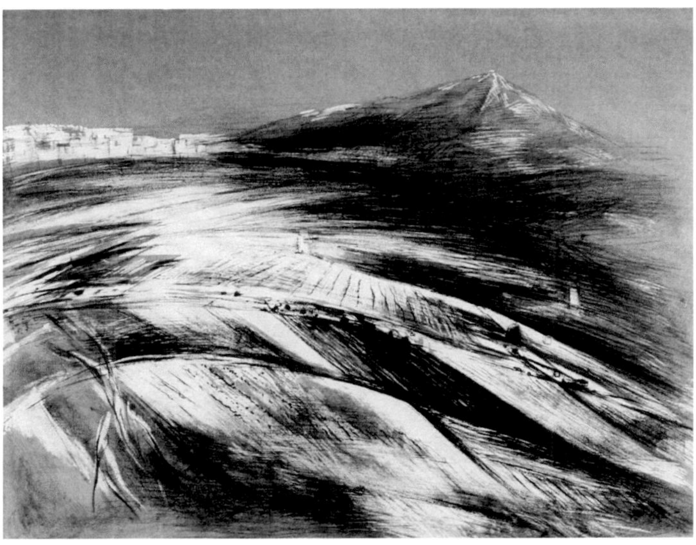

'Gozo Fields' lithograph for Curwen Press, 1977